End Time Prophecy
Simplified

Azuka Oyem

PublishAmerica
Baltimore

First printing

At the specific preference of the author, PublishAmerica allowed this work to remain exactly as the author intended, verbatim, without editorial input.

ISBN: 1-4241-5558-4
PUBLISHED BY PUBLISHAMERICA, LLLP
www.publishamerica.com
Baltimore

Printed in the United States of America

Dedicated to God
through whom all things are possible.

Contents

Introduction 7

Jesus Christ in Revelation 9

The Rapture 17

Judgment Seat of Christ 21

The Marriage of the Lamb 25

The Tribulation 31

The Four Riders of the Apocalypse 37

The Nether Regions 41

The Antichrist 45

The False Prophet 49

The Dragon 51

Michael the Archangel 57

The Twenty-Four Elders 59

The Two Witnesses 61

The 144000 Jewish Witnesses 65

The Three "Woes" of Revelation 67

The Harlot Riding the Beast and the Great City 73

Armageddon 77

The Second Coming of Christ 81

The Millennium 87

The Final Rebellion 93

The Great White Throne Judgment 95

Heaven (The Eternal State) 99

End Notes 103

Introduction

Until recent years, Bible prophecy has been considered taboo in many churches. And while many preachers will teach on salvation, financial literacy according to the Word of God, abstinence from sin and keeping the Ten Commandments, few rarely teach about the consummation of the end times even today. The general perception of the book of Revelation is that although it is immensely fascinating, full of vivid imagery, brimming with spectacular symbols and characters, it is very difficult to comprehend. Many are unsure of how to approach the book—should the passages be taken literally at face value or are they symbolic?

Yet to read the Bible and omit this last book would be a great injustice to one's self, for no story or doctrine has any meaning without an understanding of its end. This is why the book of Revelation and biblical prophecy must be studied so that there can be an awareness by every single person in the world concerning the events that must take place in the near future. The book of Revelation is the last fiber knitting all the puzzling pieces of the preceding books and ushers the whole of God's Word into a platform in which sense and understanding can be derived. Without this book, no believer can possess a mature understanding of scripture, nor can one really know Christ since His purpose and character is presented in a way not disclosed in the Old Testament nor even in the gospels.

More and more, prophecy is unfolding in our generation as humanity and creation careen towards the conclusion of this age. There are so many signs pointing to the return of Christ that only the spiritually inept can live from day to day in deceitful ignorance under the belief that this world will continue as it has always done eternally, in subjection to man's government. That is why I have written this book—to document the events that will take place very soon in a manner that is easily understood so that whoever reads this can be prepared for all that will surely come to fulfillment according to the Bible.

Jesus Christ in Revelation

Appearance of Christ

The book of Revelation is about unveiling the deity of God in Christ. It unmasks the nature of Jesus after His death and ascension to heaven, portraying Him in ways not previously seen in the preceding books of the Bible. The first point of difference is the appearance of Christ in this book in comparison to the gospels. In the gospels, Jesus was portrayed as a suffering servant who could not even be identified or distinguished from His apostles in the Garden of Gethsemane until Judas betrayed Him with a kiss. We see His painful ordeals and persecutions at the hands of the Jews and the Romans, culminating in His crucifixion and death. His weakness is prevalent throughout these gospels, showing that although He possessed the authority of God, He also bore the handicaps of humanity. In fact the book of Isaiah tells us that "He has no form or comeliness", also that "there is no beauty in Him that we should desire Him", and finally that He is a man of "sorrows and acquainted with grief" (Is 53:2-3). This is the general impression of Christ that we receive from the gospels at the time of His life upon the earth, but His appearance in Revelation is radically different.

Rev 1:13-17

And in the midst of the seven lampstands One like the Son of Man, clothed with a garment down to the feet and girded about the chest with a golden band. His head and hair were white like wool, as white as snow, and His eyes like a flame of fire; His feet were like fine brass as if refined in a furnace and His voice as the sound of many waters; He had in His right hand seven stars, out of His mouth went a sharp two-edged sword, and His countenance was like the sun shining in its strength. And when I saw Him, I fell at His feet as dead...

Never in the gospels is Christ described like this, with the exception of His transfiguration and possibly His ascension to heaven. John, the Revelator, who wrote this book, had been with Jesus during the period of His ministry on earth, but when He sees Jesus, he "falls down at His feet as dead". Why? This is because he has not seen Jesus in this glorified form before and is so shocked by what he sees that he could no longer stand on his feet! The description of Christ's garment speaks of kingly dignity; later on we are told that this garment has inscriptions which read "king of kings and lord of lords" (Rev 19:16). His hair is white as snow, not gray, indicating the fullness of life within them, and His eyes being like fire symbolizes an awareness and consciousness that defies human reasoning, out of which everything in the universe is revealed to Him in unimaginable clarity (see Heb 4:13). The description of His voice being like the sound of many waters and a sword coming out of His mouth (see Heb 4:12) reminds us of the power of His words by which He spoke the whole universe into existence. John sees His countenance dazzle with divine glory, which would have made the Jews more inclined to receive Him had His visage been like this at the time He revealed in the book of John that He is the light of the world (Jn 8:12). Throughout Revelation, Jesus is conveyed as being full of light as a proof of His divinity, having been told in earlier scripture verses that God is light and in Him there is no darkness at all (1 Jn 1:5). He radiates so much light that in the eternal state there will be no need for a sun or moon.

Rev 21:23-24

The city had no need of the sun or of the moon to shine in it, for the glory of God illuminated it. The Lamb is its light. And the nations of those who are saved shall walk in its light, and the kings of the earth bring their glory and honor into it.

Names of Jesus

He is given names in the book of Revelation to describe Him in such a way as to make the reader understand Him for who He really is and the role He plays as both Savior of the believer and as the God of the universe. He is called the "Son of Man" by John, identifying his conception and descent from the line of men, as well as denoting His Godship and the authority that comes with this title, as was prophesied in the book of Daniel.

Daniel 7:13-14

"I was watching in the night visions, and behold, One like the Son of Man, coming with the clouds of heaven! He came to the Ancient of Days, and they brought Him near before Him. Then to Him was given dominion and glory and a kingdom, that all peoples, nations, and languages should serve Him. His dominion is an everlasting dominion, which shall not pass away and His kingdom the one which shall not be destroyed.

The Son of Man was also Christ's own popular address of Himself during His time on earth. He is also called the Lamb to depict His humility and gentleness. Coupled with the words "I am He who lives; and was dead, and behold I am alive forevermore" (Rev 1:18) we are reminded that He was led as a lamb to the slaughter. Just as animals were killed to atone for sins in the Old Testament, so was Jesus offered up as a perfect sacrifice for the sins of the world. His nature is like that of a lamb—quiet and unimposing, which is why He tells us that He stands at the door of our hearts knocking, waiting for us to open up to Him, rather than entering in uninvited (Rev 3:20).

Rev 5:6
And I looked, and behold, in the midst of the throne and of the four living creatures, and in the midst of the elders, stood a Lamb as though it had been slain, having seven horns and seven eyes, which are the seven Spirits of God sent out into all the earth.

He is called the "Bridegroom" to show the role He plays concerning the church. He has an everlasting covenant of fellowship with the church; He purchased her, died for her and will receive her to Himself so that He and the church will dwell together throughout all eternity. From the onset of His appearance in Revelation, He immediately begins to address the church. In later passages, we see the church preparing herself for marriage to the Bridegroom.

Rev 19:7-8
"Let us be glad and rejoice and give Him glory, for the marriage of the Lamb has come, and His wife has made herself ready." And to her it was granted to be arrayed in fine linen, clean and bright, for the fine linen is the righteous acts of the saints.

Jesus is called the "Word of God" suggesting that not only does He proceed from His Father, He is equal to his Father. This is John's favorite title for Jesus in his gospel, asserting that, "In the beginning was the Word, and the Word was with God, and the Word was God" (Jn 1:1). He declares that Jesus existed before His incarnation, proclaiming that, "the Word became flesh and dwelt among us" (Jn 1:14). We are also told in John's epistle that "there are three that bear witness in heaven: the Father, the Word, and the Holy Spirit; and these three are one" (1 Jn 5:7).

Rev 19:12-13
His eyes were like a flame of fire, and on His head were many crowns. He had a name written that no one knew except Himself. He was clothed with a robe dipped in blood, and His name is called The Word of God.

Here is a list of Christ's own declarations of Himself in Revelation:

- Alpha and Omega (Rev 1:8)
- The beginning and the end (Rev 1:8; 22:13)
- Who is, who was and who is to come (Rev 1:8)
- The first and the last (Rev 1:11,17; 2:8; 22:13)
- He who lives, and was dead and am alive forevermore (Rev 1:18; 2:8)
- He who has the sharp two-edged sword (Rev 2:12)
- The Son of God (Rev 2:18)
- He who has eyes like a flame of fire and feet like brass (Rev 2:18)
- He who has the seven Spirits of God and the seven stars (Rev 3:1)
- He who is holy and true (Rev 3:7)
- He who has the key of David (Rev 3:7)
- He who opens and no one shuts (Rev 3:7)
- The Amen, the Faithful and True Witness (Rev 3:14)
- The Beginning of the creation of God (Rev 3:14)
- The Root and Offspring of David (Rev 22:16)
- The Bright and Morning Star (Rev 22:16)

His Authority

Jesus is pictured as an authoritative figure in the book of Revelation, and rightly so since He is the protagonist of this prophetic writings just as the devil is the antagonist. Just in the first few verses of the first chapter of this book alone, there are numerous references to 'His' (such as *His* servant, John, *His* angels etc.) suggesting ownership and an authority which extends beyond that which a created being can of itself possess. John sees Him walking between the golden lamp stands (Rev 1:13) and being in the midst of the elders (Rev 5:6) to emphasize Christ's presence among the church. His holding seven stars (Rev 1:16) show ownership of the angels watching over the churches (see Rev 1:20).

He has authority not only to give life to the dead (Rev 20:4) but also to execute judgment. In fact, the notion of His judgments are a prominent one in this book. We are given an insight into the condemnation of the ungodly at the Great White Throne judgment, in which the unbelievers since Adam shall stand before Him awaiting His sentence into the lake of fire (see Rev 20:11-15). At this judgment, it is clear that we are not dealing with a mere man for the "earth and heaven" fled away from His face demonstrating the awesomeness of the wrath of God. John weeps when no one is counted worthy to open the scroll, but Christ as God emerges from among the saints, doing what no created being can do by opening the seals. His opening the seals show that He is in control of the judgments which occur during the tribulation period.

Rev 5:7-9
Then He came and took the scroll out of the right hand of Him who sat on the throne. Now when He had taken the scroll, the four living creatures and the twenty-four elders fell down before the Lamb, each having a harp, and golden bowls full of incense, which are the prayers of the saints. And they sang a new song, saying: "You are worthy to take the scroll, and to open its seals; for You were slain, and have redeemed us to God by Your word out of every tribe and tongue and people and nation."

The Promises of Jesus

His promises in this book of prophecy are centered on the church, just as are his loving reproaches and suggestions of improvement. There are numerous rewards that He promises the church, but also warns explicitly that to receive them, the church must "overcome" or "endure to the end". Here is a list of Christ's promises to those who overcome:

- They will eat of the tree of life (Rev 2:7)
- They shall not be hurt by the second death (Rev 2:11)
- They will eat some of the hidden manna (Rev 2:17)
- They will receive a new name written on a stone (Rev 2:17)
- They will be given power over the nations (Rev 2:26)
- They will be given the morning star (Rev 2:28)
- They shall be clothed in white garments (Rev 3:5)
- Their names shall not be blotted out of the book of life (Rev 3:12)

- They will be made pillars in the temple of God (Rev 3:12)
- They will have Christ's new name written on them (Rev 3:12)
- They will be granted the privilege of seating with Christ on His throne (Rev 3:21)

The notion of the Second Coming of Christ is prevalent in the book of Revelation. We are told from the first verses that the time of the unfolding of the last-days events are "near" (Rev 1:3). Christ Himself over-emphasizes His soon coming return throughout this book more than anyone else. This is because of the urgency of His message—we have little time before He returns and so we should persevere in obedience to Him and endure the evils of this age because it is only for a short period. Jesus does not dilate His words but asserts firmly that He *will* come again (see Rev 3:11; 16:15; 22:7; 22:20)

Rev 22:12

"And behold, I am coming quickly, and My reward is with Me, to give to every one according to his work. I am the Alpha and Omega, the Beginning and the End, the First and the Last."

The Rapture

The word "rapture" doesn't actually exist in the Bible, it is derived from the Greek word "harpazo", which means to "snatch" or "seize" suddenly. In Latin, it is "rapio", and when translated to the English language we are given the word "rapture". It is the next major prophetic event on God's calendar. In fact, it is the first stage of the second coming of Jesus Christ in which he returns to earth to gather church-age believers to himself and take them to the Father's house. There are two key passages that reveal this event:

1 Thessalonians 4:16
The Lord himself will descend from heaven with a shout, with the voice of an archangel and with the trumpet of God and the dead in Christ will rise first. And we who are alive and remain shall be caught up together with them in the clouds to meet the Lord in the air. And thus we shall always be with the Lord.

1 Corinthians 15:51
Behold, I tell you a mystery, we shall not all sleep but we shall all be changed. In a moment, in the twinkling of an eye, at the last trumpet. For the trumpet will sound and the dead will be raised incorruptible, and we shall be changed. For this corruptible must put on incorruption, and this mortal must put on immortality.

At the rapture, Jesus Christ will return in the air (notice that he does not actually alight on the earth) and all dead believers who are in Christ will be resurrected and, along with those who are alive at the time of this first phase of his second coming, will be snatched up to meet Him in the air. Then He will take us to Heaven where we will forever be with Him. This means that some Christians are never going to taste death! Those who are alive shall be changed into their glorified bodies in the time that it takes to blink an eye.

The rapture will occur rapidly. In such a short period of time, Christ seizes his own out of the world and from its systems to be with Him. It is a sign-less event, which means that there are no signs which must take place before it occurs or clues indicating its approach. It is imminent—it can take place at any moment. Jesus himself often declared that he would return for his people, stating also that he would return at a time that "no one knows".

The sudden and inexplicable disappearance of Christians will usher the world into a state of chaos. Headlines and the media will have field days documenting theories and articles of the simultaneous reports of vast numbers of missing-persons. Many individuals will actually witness a friend, a relative or unknown person suddenly rise into the sky with no explanation of what they will see. Imagine the scenario of students in a classroom who are shocked to discover that their teacher has vanished from sight in their presence. Fear will overtake the nations of the world on a scale yet unseen in our present day.

Again, I want to clarify that not everyone will be privileged to experience the rapture, and not *all* believers shall partake in it. Only church-age believers—those since the day of Pentecost until the occurrence of the rapture shall be taken in this first phase of the Second Coming. Old Testament believers will be resurrected and receive their glorified bodies at the end of the tribulation and not at the rapture. We are presently in the church age, otherwise known as the age of grace, which in my opinion is the best dispensation of all the time periods until the millennial age, which shall be discussed later on in this book. Here is a list of events from creation to the eternal state:

1. Creation
2. Old Testament age
3. Church age
4. Rapture
5. Tribulation
6. Second coming of Christ
7. Millennium
8. Eternal state

Paul describes the rapture as a "mystery". In the Bible, a mystery is not something that is mysterious or puzzling, a mystery is a concept that has not been previously revealed up until that moment when it is unraveled. Therefore, the rapture is a mystery because it had not been mentioned in the scriptures until the New Testament.

The Purpose for the Rapture

In the book of John 14:2, Jesus said that He goes to prepare a place for us and that if He goes He will also return to receive us to Himself. These very words were uttered from the lips of our Savior and validate the authenticity of the rapture. Jesus will return to take His beloved bride— the church—to heaven so that we might always be with Him. At the present, Christ is in heaven preparing a place for every believer in His Father's house, and has been doing so since His ascension to heaven— about the last two thousand years!

The purpose of the rapture is also to end the present age of grace and begin the time of judgment upon the earth. The world is still operational, and the natural balance of the elements are yet unperturbed because of the presence of the church on the earth. While the church exists in our world today, there cannot be global catastrophes the likes of which are mentioned of during the tribulation because God's favor abounds on the earth while there are those in which He has given His Spirit to residing therein. This is why any who hold the position of the mid-tribulation rapture or the post-tribulation rapture is in opposition to the coherent doctrine of the scriptures. Only the doctrine that the rapture must precede the tribulation is the correct one since it is in alignment with the character of God.

All through the scriptures, we see that God does not judge a nation without first removing the Godly from the destruction that He has scheduled. Before the judgment of Sodom and Gomorrah, Lot was advised to flee because destruction could not be unleashed from God while he remained there. Abraham was bold enough to ask the pre-incarnate Jesus if he would destroy Sodom and Gomorrah if there were ten good men there, and Jesus answered "no" (see Gen 18:22-33). In our world today, there are more than ten righteous men so God cannot begin the tribulation until He has vacated those who love Him. Here are some scriptures that support this teaching.

1 Thess 5:9

For God did not appoint us to wrath but to obtain salvation through our Lord Jesus Christ.

Rev 3:10

Because you have kept my command to persevere, I also will keep you from the hour of trial that shall come upon the whole world, to test those who dwell on the earth.

The tribulation is the time of God's wrath, but this is directed at the sinners dwelling on the earth, not believers. The church of Philadelphia described in Revelation chapter 3:7-12 typifies the true believers among the church that shall be raptured because they have kept the commands of God.

Another proof that the church is raptured before the tribulation is the fact that nothing is mentioned of them during the turmoil of the tribulation. Why? This is because they have been taken to heaven and are rejoicing with Christ.

Judgment Seat of Christ

While the tribulation begins on earth shortly after the rapture, the saints (believers) will be in heaven with the Savior. Firstly, every believer will be judged for the things done in the flesh (2 Cor 5:10) and we must give an account of the way we have lived our lives here on the earth. All of our deeds are recorded in heaven and the motives behind our actions will be disclosed. Our intentions, whether good or bad, and our secret endeavors will be brought to light (1 Cor 4:5).

Heb 4:13
And there is no creature hidden from His sight but all things are naked and open to the eyes of Him to whom we must give account.

Jesus Christ is the judge (Jn 5:22), and the purpose of the judgment is not to decide whether or not we are fit for heaven. Once a person accepts Jesus Christ as their personal Savior in this lifetime, he has already "passed from death unto life" (Jn 5:24) so this moment is not an opportunistic moment for Christ to show us our sins to condemn us as some people think, for the Bible explicitly says that there is no condemnation for those who walk in the Spirit and not according to the flesh (Rom 8:1), and again that the blood of Jesus washes us from all sin (1 Jn 1:7). The purpose of the judgment seat of Christ is to determine what rewards we shall receive for the works we do on the earth. There will be a variance in the degree of rewards; those who commit their lives to obeying God, keeping his word and endeavoring in the work of God, even at their own expense, will receive greater rewards than those who are "lay" Christians—who are dedicated to living a life only partially committed to the Lord, Jesus Christ. The parable in Luke 19:13-26 is to be taken literally, for those who are committed to God in this life shall be given many cities to rule over in the next life, while those Christians who are reluctant to live to the standard of purity and holiness shall rule over only a few cities.

How the Judgment Is Carried out at the Judgment Seat

The judgment seat of Christ should not be considered insignificant in the light that this judgment is not to determine our entrance into heaven or hell, for it shall nevertheless be an intense scrutiny of every single action ever carried out by the individual with excruciating detail so that the facts of the believer's life are indisputable. Regardless of whether the details have eluded the believer's memory, it does not elude Christ's. His eyes are a "flame of fire" (Rev 1:14). He is omniscient (knows all things) and judges with righteousness (Rev 19:11). His judgment is impartial; he does not indulge in favoritism, but according to what we have done only does He review.

Romans 14:10-12
...for we shall all stand before the judgment seat of Christ for it is written "As I live, says the Lord, every knee shall bow to Me, and every tongue shall confess to God."

We shall give an account for every single word we have ever uttered (Matt 12:36) because our words create our destiny and spiritual environment and declares the kind of heart we have. Our nature, whether good or bad, are declared through the medium of speech. You can learn a great deal about a person's character by simply listening to a conversation they engage in.

Proverbs 10:11 states that: *The mouth of the righteous is a well of life, but violence covers the mouth of the wicked.*

Believers who use profane words liberally or use the name of the Lord in vain will one day be brought before God concerning it. Even our thoughts shall be reviewed to see what engages our minds—the things of God or the things of the world. Jesus said that whoever lusts after a woman in his mind has already committed a sin (Matt 5:28). Repeatedly, Paul urges us to have the same mind that Jesus has and also to renew it (Rom 12:2). We are to "meditate" on God's Word day and night (Josh 1:8) and seek first God's kingdom and righteousness (Matt 6:33).

We may fool others by assuming an appearance of divine holiness, but God cannot be fooled or "mocked" (Gal 6:7) He knows what we do and why we do it, and bases His reward on the legitimacy of our deeds. Many people we revere now may not receive great rewards, and those we have overlooked may reap "treasures in heaven".

Our treatment of others and our attitude towards the nation of Israel will be looked upon. Our zeal to carry out the Great Commission (win souls for Christ) will also be studied among other things. Much will be expected from leaders and teachers of the Word. How exactly God carries out His judgment on each believer is revealed in this passage of scripture.

1 Cor 3: 13-15

Each one's work will become clear, for the Day will declare it, because it will be revealed by fire, and the fire will test each one's work, of what sort it is. If anyone's work which he has built on it endures, he will receive a reward. If anyone's work is burned, he will suffer loss; but he himself will be saved, yet so as through fire.

Whether this passage is to be taken to be literal fire is debatable, but, nonetheless, the indication is that our works will pass through a testing mechanism, of which our works will either remain and we shall be given a reward or they will be burned if our motives were despicable. Notice again that the Christian will be "saved, yet through fire", which implies that our salvation is not negotiated by works but our rewards in heaven are. On the judgment day, some will be grievously ashamed while others will rejoice for their active duty and service to God in this life.

We shall also receive crowns on the judgment day as part of the rewards for this present life. Then indeed it shall be evident to all that we are kings and priests unto God (1 Pet 2:9).

The Marriage
of the Lamb

The church is the bride of Christ. Every believer since the day of Pentecost until the rapture is a member of the church, and thereby a component of the body that constitutes the bride. God created marriage. Even from the genesis of Adam, he created Eve for the purpose of instituting a marriage bond between the two. Throughout the scriptures, we read of the laws that a marriage couple must follow and we are shown how seriously God views marriage. God says that what He has put together let no one "rend asunder" because a marriage is suppose to be an indestructible bond that continues for the lifetime of the parties involved. Under no circumstances is there to be a divorce (Mark 10:9) only in the case of infidelity can a divorce be carried out; or only at death should there be a separation of the married couple. In our modern life, the institution of marriage has become a charade in which one can enter into easily and exit quickly, or even remarry again according to how each individual pleases. Among the celebrities of Hollywood particularly, marriage is perceived as a fashion trend that is en vogue today and out of taste tomorrow, so that there is a lack of commitment attitude to a majority of those who do not understand the concept of a marriage.

God is so occupied with marriage because He wants to set the example among men of the coming marriage that will take place in heaven in which the true bride and the true Bridegroom shall dwell together forever in perfect unity with each other. In the weddings of men, there are several stages and elements involved that makes up a marriage, and likewise the marriage of the Lamb and the bride also has procedures. To understand the marriage of the Lamb, it is wise to first identify the participants in this marriage.

The host of the marriage is God, the Father. He is the father of the bridegroom. He plans out the marriage and ensures that all the vital elements for the wedding are in place. He selects the bride carefully for His Son (see Jn 15:1-2) and sends out invitations.

Matt 22:1-2

And Jesus answered and spoke to them again by parables and said "The kingdom of heaven is like a certain king who arranged a marriage for his son."

In Israel and certain parts of the Arabic world, the first step to a marriage is the selection of the bride by the father of the bridegroom. After careful observations and consultations with the son and the mother, he arrives at his conclusion. The Bible declares that before the world was created, God chose a bride for His Son (Eph 1:4).

The bridegroom is Jesus, the only begotten Son of God. He is referred to as "the Lamb" in the book of Revelation not only as a reflection of His humble character but as a reminder of the sacrifice He paid for all humanity. In English literature, through the use of fictional characters, a wedding is often portrayed as the husband "purchasing" the bride, and even now it is sometimes perceived that the bride belongs to the bridegroom. Certainly, a married woman changes her last name to that of her husband's, she is taken into his house and he becomes her lord; so likewise Jesus "purchased" us with His shed blood on Calvary that we might be His. And as a woman is told to submit to her husband, so also are we to submit to Christ (Eph 5:24). Jesus describes Himself as the bridegroom in Luke 5:34 when asked by the Scribes and the Pharisees why it was that He mingled with the tax collectors and sinners.

Just as a ring is given to the bride-to-be until the time of the wedding, so also has Christ given the Holy Spirit to his bride—the church—as a confirmation of His devotion to her until the time He comes to claim her in marriage. It is through the Spirit of God that the church is qualified and sanctified to be called the bride, and He assures us of our absolute salvation in our Lord.

Eph 1:13,14
In Him you trusted, after you heard the word of truth, the gospel of your salvation: in whom also, having believed, you were sealed with the Holy Spirit of promise, who is the guarantee of our inheritance until the redemption of the purchased possession, to the praise of His glory.

This church age is the betrothal stage, in which the church awaits her husband's return to whisk her to the wedding. There is no knowledge to be contracted as to when Jesus will return and so in the meantime the bride must wait in eager anticipation, keeping herself pure with the help of the Holy Spirit dwelling in her until the time of the return of Jesus Christ. Jesus promised that just as He would ascend to heaven after His resurrection, He would also return to receive His church.

Jn 14:1
Let not your heart be troubled; you believe in God, believe also in Me. In My Father's house are many mansions; if it were not so I would have told you. I go to prepare a place for you. And if I go and prepare a place for you, I will come again and receive you to Myself; that where I am, there you may be also.

Jesus, the Bridegroom, desires uninterrupted fellowship with the church. He left heaven to woo her, satisfying the statement that "therefore a man shall leave his Father and mother and be joined to his wife, and they shall become one flesh" (Gen 2:24). The church shall be conformed to the image of the Son of God (Rom 8:29) and receive a glorified body so that we shall attain the highest fellowship and intimacy with Christ.

At any wedding, the bride's appearance is paramount to the success of the day, but what shall the church wear on her wedding day? Rev 19:8 has the answer. This passage of scripture reveals that all believers will be arrayed in fine linen, and the material of the linen is the righteous acts of the saints. This means that although we are not accepted into heaven based on the works we do on earth (since believing and confessing the Lord Jesus Christ is enough) our apparel on the wedding day will dazzle according to the works done on earth. Your actions every day are sewing your wedding garment. How stunning you look at the marriage of the Lamb in front of our Lord and the other believers is already being put in place by what you are doing right now.

Rev 19:7-9

"Let us be glad and rejoice and give Him glory, for the marriage of the Lamb has come, and His wife has made herself ready." And to her it was granted to be arrayed in fine linen, clean and bright, for the fine linen is the righteous acts of the saints.

In Israel, once the betrothal time-period has ended, the father of the bridegroom sends his son to bring the bride to his dwelling place. The marriage ceremony consists mainly in "taking" the bride. It is common for a torch-lit procession to come during the night to the residence of the bride. Once there, the father of the bride places her hand in the bridegroom's "presenting" her to him. Then the procession will head back to the father's house where a feast awaited them in which the groom's father had invited friends. To decline an invitation is an open insult to the family. Soon, the Father in heaven is going to tell the Son to go and get His bride, and the saints shall be raptured into heaven to the Father's house where Christ has been preparing a place for us for two thousand years. Then the saints will celebrate greatly until the time of Christ's second coming with His believers unto the earth at the end of the tribulation. The heavenly Father will then throw a party for the Bridegroom, which lasts for a thousand years. Those that survive the tribulation and are considered worthy to enter the coming millennium will be invitees along with the friends of Christ (the Old Testament saints and tribulation martyrs) who will be resurrected at the end of the tribulation (see Rev 20:4). John the Baptist declared himself to be the friend of Christ and not the bride since he represented the old dispensation and died before the day of Pentecost (the coming of the Holy Spirit).

Jn 3:27-29

John answered and said, "A man can receive nothing unless it has been given to him from heaven. You yourselves bear me witness that I said, 'I am not the Christ,' but, 'I have been sent before Him.' He who has the bride is the bridegroom; but the friend of the bridegroom, who stands and hears him, rejoices greatly because of the bridegroom's voice. Therefore this joy of mine is fulfilled."

The Tribulation

This is the time of the last days of the earth and its systems as we know it. It is a time of absolute hell on earth; of disaster and chaos and wrath as has not been experienced since creation began. The horrors of the tribulation are such that Christ must rapture the church from the earth so that we do not partake in this time of judgment. The word "tribulation" denotes "hardship" as derived from trouble. Webster's pocket dictionary describes tribulation as "great distress or suffering caused by oppression". Nothing humanity has experienced will compare to the time of the tribulation. Hiroshima, the Black Plague, Hitler's tyranny, and more recently the attack on the World Trade Center and hurricanes Katrina, Rita and Beta will seem insignificant in the light of the cataclysmic upheavals that shall come upon the earth. Joel 2:2 assert that it is "a day of darkness and gloominess, a day of clouds and thick darkness". Here are some other scripture verses that discuss how terrible the tribulation will be.

Jer 30:7
Alas! For that day is great, so that none is like it; and it is the time of Jacob's trouble, but he shall be saved out of it.

Dan 12:1

At that time Michael shall stand up, the great prince who stands watch over the sons of your people; and there shall be a time of trouble, such as never was since there was a nation even to that time. And at that time your people shall be delivered, every one who is found written in the book.

Matt 24:21-22

For then there will be great tribulation, such as has not been since the beginning of the world until this time, no, nor ever shall be. And unless those days were shortened, no flesh would be saved; but for the elect's sake those days will be shortened.

Remarkable! Three different passages of scripture, from three different time periods and three different sources, yet all saying the same thing. There will never be a time of worldwide devastation and severe oppression like that which occurs in the duration of the tribulation. Since the tribulation covers the "whole world" no creature will be unaffected by it and the earth as well as the stellar heavens (outer space) will be shaken to the core.

The tribulation officially begins when the Antichrist signs a peace treaty with Israel. Nothing is mentioned of exactly how many days, months or years that elapses between the rapture and the beginning of the tribulation in the Bible, but since the Antichrist rises to power so quickly it cannot be too long. The duration of the tribulation is seven years; it begins with the Antichrist signing the peace treaty with Israel and ends with the second coming of Jesus Christ. In his visions, Daniel the prophet is told that seventy weeks are determined for Israel to end universal sin (Dan 9:24) and at the end of the seventieth week Christ would "bring in everlasting righteousness" and set up His kingdom on earth physically at His second coming. A "week" being seven years, it should have taken 490 years (70X7) from the time of Daniel's vision to the time of the second coming. However, there is an interval between weeks 69 and 70, which is the church age. It appears that because of the Jews rejection of Christ, God "stops" the clock momentarily on the Jews and focuses on the Gentiles—the church. The church age is referred to as a "mystery" because it was hidden from the writers of the Old Testament. Presently, we live in this interval, but the clock will begin again after the saints are raptured, and God will again direct His focus prominently on Israel. The tribulation is described as the "seventieth week". Here is a list of other names to describe the tribulation.

- The time of the end (Dan 12:9)
- The day of the Lord (1 Thess 5:2,4)
- The hour of trial (Rev 3:10)
- The wrath of the Lamb (Rev 6:16)
- The great and dreadful day of the Lord (Mal 4:5)
- A day of devastation and desolation (Zeph 1:15)
- The hour of judgment (Rev 14:7)

This seven-year period is divided into two equal halves of three and a half years. The first three and a half years are generally called "the tribulation" while the last three and a half years are referred to as 'the great tribulation'. The final half of the tribulation (known as a time, times and half a time, 42 months or 1260 days) begins when the Antichrist breaks his treaty of peace with Israel, invades her and sets up an image of himself in the temple.

Dan 9:27

Then he shall confirm a covenant with many for one week; but in the middle of the week he shall bring an end to sacrifice and offering. And on the wing of abominations shall be one who makes desolate, even until the consummation which is determined, is poured out on the desolate.

The tribulation period is clearly the time of God's judgment. He is in control of the unseemingly uncontrollable chaos manifested on the earth. With the church safely in heaven, God pours out His wrath in three waves throughout the tribulation.

The Seven Seal Judgments

1. White horse—the world's greatest dictator.
2. Red horse—the world's greatest war.
3. Black horse—the world's greatest famine.
4. Pale horse—the world's greatest death count.
5. Martyrs in heaven—the world's greatest persecution of believers.
6. Universal devastation—the world's greatest ecological disasters.
7. Seven trumpet judgments—heaven's silence and the world's greatest hour of fear.

The Seven Trumpet Judgments

1. Hail and fire mingled with blood—the world's greatest fire.
2. Fireball from heaven—the world's greatest oceanic disturbance.
3. Burning star from heaven—the world's greatest pollution of water.
4. One-third of sun, stars and moon darkened—the world's greatest darkness.
5. Demonic invasion—the world's greatest hour of pain.
6. Demonic army which kills one-third of mankind—the world's greatest army.
7. The announcement of Christ's reign—the world's greatest storm.

The Seven Bowl Judgments

1. Sores on the Antichrist's worshippers—the world's greatest plague.
2. Seas turn to blood—the world's greatest ocean of blood.
3. Rivers and springs of water turn to blood—the world's greatest contamination by blood.
4. Intense heat from the sun—the world's greatest scorching.
5. Darkness upon the Antichrist's kingdom—the world's greatest blasphemy towards God.

6. River Euphrates dries up—the world's greatest invasion at Armageddon.

7. The air filled with lightnings and thunderings—the world's greatest earthquake.

From the descriptions of these unparalleled disasters, it is easy to create a portrait in our minds of the coming troubles upon the earth. But what is the purpose of the tribulation? Certainly, God has a reasonable answer for everything He does and one purpose the tribulation serves is to bring Israel to its knees in repentance so that they again return to the true God of their fathers. The Jews were so preoccupied with their legalistic religion that when God reached down to them in the form of Jesus Christ they did not recognize Him as their Messiah. But in the time of their immeasurable oppression, when deliverance cannot be found on earth, they will call out to God once more. Previous Jewish holocausts will appear insignificant in comparison to the oppression of Israel during the last days, so much so that only one-third of the Jews survive the tribulation. In fact, for the sake of the Jewish nation, the tribulation has been shortened to only seven years (Matt 24:22).

Zech 13:8-9

"And it shall come to pass in all the land," says the Lord, "that two-thirds in it shall be cut off and die, but one-third shall be left in it: I will bring the one-third through the fire, will refine them as silver is refined, and test them as gold is tested. They will call on My name, and I will answer them. I will say, 'This is My people'; and each one will say, 'The Lord is my God.'"

Along with the Jews turning their hearts to God, countless people will be saved in the midst of so colossal an affliction. Many theologists believe that once an individual is unfortunate to partake in the rapture, he is not going to be given a second chance to receive salvation, due to 2 Thess 2:11,12 which suggests that God will delude the minds of those left behind into believing the lies of the Antichrist. However, God is a god of second chances and will receive any who turn to Him. Acts 2:21 declares that whoever shall call upon the name of the Lord shall be saved, and the context of this verse is certainly during the tribulation period because the preceding verse (Act 2:20) speaks of the sun being darkened and the moon turning to blood. In addition to this, John sees the souls of those who had been slain for the Word of God under the altar. These are martyrs who were converted during the tribulation period and died for their faith.

Rev 7:9,14

After these things I looked, and behold, a great multitude which no one could number, of all nations, tribes, people, and tongues, standing before the throne and before the Lamb...these are the ones who come out of the great tribulation, and washed their robes and made them white in the blood of the Lamb.

The tribulation period discloses the true character of Satan. With the church gone and the "hinderer" removed, who is the Holy Spirit dwelling in believers' hearts (see 2 Thess 2:7), then Satan's nature is revealed in a way not seen prior to the book of Revelation. He is a counterfeiter, a blasphemer, and a destructive force that yearns worship. Realizing that his time in the limelight has come and that it will be short, he unleashes his venom upon the whole world and on the Jews with a ferocity yet unseen up until that moment.

Rev 12:12

"Therefore rejoice, o heavens, and you who dwell in them! Woe to the inhabitants of the earth and the sea! For the devil has come down to you, having great wrath, because he knows that he has a short time."

The tribulation also serves as a tool in which God punishes the world for rejecting His Son. He manifests His power to the Antichrist, who declares himself as God, and also rains judgments on this villain and his kingdom of darkness.

The Four Riders
of the Apocalypse

As a child, when I read the book of Revelation and came across the riders mentioned in chapter 6, they appeared so ominous and full of power that I felt obliged to understand who or what they were. Since they are the first seals unleashed on the earth, and are pictured on horses, these riders are captains leading the way for the other devastations that will follow, and they are prevalent figures throughout the tribulation.

Rev 6:2
And I looked, and behold, a white horse. He who sat on it had a bow; and a crown was given to him, and he went out conquering and to conquer.

This is clearly not Christ since He is in heaven opening the seal judgments. Christ comes to the earth on a white horse at the end of the tribulation. This rider is the Antichrist who enters the world scene as a conqueror going out to conquer. He is pictured as a white rider because during the uproar of the disappearance of many Christians as a result of the rapture, he steps into the political podium declaring peace and even signs a peace treaty with Israel. Being seated on a horse represents the speed in which he rises to power and takes over nations. He is a false Christ, wearing a crown which signifies rulership. His possessing a "bow" but no mention of arrows suggests that although possessing military armament, he conquers primarily through deception.

Rev 6:3

When He opened the second seal, I heard the second living creature saying, "Come and see." Another horse, fiery red, went out. And it was granted to the one who sat on it to take peace from the earth, and that people should kill one another; and there was given to him a great sword.

This rider is figurative and represents war, which is the result of the Antichrist going forth conquering. Peace is removed from the earth and wars break out. Jesus Himself reminds us that in the end times, nation will rise against nation and there will be wars and rumors of wars (Matt 24:6,7). The "sword" represents murder and bloodshed. This indicates that there will not only be wars but social unrest also, racial homicide, labor strikes, individual feuds and a general state of emergency.

Rev 6:5

When He opened the third seal, I heard the third living creature say, "Come and see." So I looked, and behold, a black horse, and he who sat on it had a pair of scales in his hand. And I heard a voice in the midst of the four living creatures saying, "A quart of wheat for a denarius, and three quarts of barley for a denarius; and do not harm the oil and the wine."

The black horse represents famine, which swiftly follows after war. In our contemporary world, we measure food items such as tomatoes by their weight in pounds to decide how much their value are. A denarius is probably about a day's wages, which suggests that the value of foods will increase so much that every penny of wages earned will be spent on foods. Anyone who possessed products such as oil and wine stands to make a small fortune because the rich requires such items. Hence, those who are poor are at higher risk of starvation than the wealthy. Today, we complain of inflation when we review the price of gasoline or certain products, but during the tribulation there will be a global economic decline that has not occurred in any previous generation.

Rev 6:8

So I looked, and behold, a pale horse. And the name of him who sat on it was Death, and Hades followed with him. And power was given to them over a fourth of the earth, to kill with the sword, with hunger, with death, and by the beasts of the earth.

We do not have to guess who this rider is; for we are explicitly told that it is Death. Hades is the place of the unrighteous dead and since lawlessness will abound during this seven-year period, many souls who perish will quickly enter hell. When an individual suffers an ailment, we often describe them as being "pale". Death is a pale rider because of the ugly shadow it shall cast upon the earth when it kills a forth of mankind. Of course, Death is personified here; the real cause of death is mentioned in the latter part of the verse.

The Nether Regions

Among even the church, there is confusion about the after-life; more especially with scriptures pertaining to the nether regions where the souls of the damned are said to inhabit. So it is best to clarify the various compartments of hell before continuing our study of occurrences during the tribulation. These are the various places of incarceration in hell:

Sheol (Hades)

The common name for "hell" in the Old Testament is "Sheol" which means "the grave" where people went when they died. The Hebrew word "sheol" was translated in Greek as "hades". To understand this place, it is advisable to read the story in Luke 16:19-31. This is a temporary place that is divided into two compartments—paradise and torments.

Paradise—This is also called Abraham's Bosom. It is a compartment that was formally inhabited by the righteous dead in the Old Testament. Jesus told one of the men who was crucified with Him that he would be in paradise that same day, confirming the sinner's last-minute salvation. Paradise was a place of comfort (Luke 16:25). The human senses still functioned in the after-life since both parties could communicate with one another as well as see each other. There is a "great gulf fixed" between Paradise and Torments (hades), which denied access between both compartments. It appears also that Paradise was a place of fellowship since Lazarus was carried to Abraham's bosom. Paradise is now presently empty. When Jesus rose from the dead, He led the inhabitants of this compartment to heaven (Eph 4:8). The spirit and soul of a believer who dies now is automatically escorted by angels directly into heaven (2 Cor 5:8).

Torments (Hades)—This is a temporary prison for the souls of unrighteous men from all generations since Adam until the Millennium. Just as criminals are placed in jailhouses before receiving a court hearing and are then sentenced, so also are these ungodly rabble awaiting their sentence at the Great White Throne judgment. The punishment of hades is: burning; separation and loneliness since the rich man is unconscious of any other soul in hades; conviction by memory; thirst and stench. The rich man could not escape his torment. Hades is a real place; Bible scholars no longer regard this story as a parable but as an actual event that took place of which Jesus was aware of. Jesus often took his disciples aside to explain His parables afterward but no explanation is given to this story.

Tartarus

This is the place of temporary confinement for a select group of angels until they are sent to the lake of fire. These angels had left their proper domain in heaven and came to earth seeking "strange flesh" (Jude 7). 2 Pet 2:4 tells us that these particular angels had "sinned" and so God had cast them down to hell where they are confined in "everlasting chains" under darkness until the judgment. The sin of these angels is sexual in nature. Gen 6:2 expresses the lust the "sons of God" bore for the "daughters of men", and again Gen 6:4 discloses that the "sons of God" came into the daughters of men and they bore children. In the Old Testament, angels were called "sons of God" so this is clearly the angels now presently in Tartarus. Whether the angels had sexual intercourse with women or whether they tempted evil men into sexual immorality with the intent of contaminating the human race so the Christ could not emerge from such a sinful line is unclear. However, the children born to those women were giants, suggesting a supernatural co-habitation of which the occurrence of the Flood was necessary to cleanse.

The Abyss or Bottomless Pit

Also located in hell. It appears to be a place of torment for demons (fallen angels) as suggested by the encounter between Jesus and the man at the country of the Gadarenes (Luke 8:28). The demons who possessed the man seemed terrified of this place (Luke 8:31) and begged Him not to send them there. Jesus holds the authority to send these demons to the Abyss, and the church strengthened by the Holy Spirit should be able to do likewise in this age. It also appears to be an incredibly hot place for when it is opened during the tribulation, so that locust-like demons can afflict the ungodly, smoke arises out of it like "the smoke of a great furnace" (Rev 9:2). During the Millennium, Satan and his demons will be confined to the Abyss temporarily.

Rev 20:1-3

Then I saw an angel coming down from heaven, having the key to the bottomless pit and a great chain in his hand. He laid hold of the dragon, that serpent of old, who is the Devil and Satan, and bound him for a thousand years; and he cast him into the bottomless pit, and shut him up, and set a seal on him, so that he should deceive the nations no more till the thousand years were finished. But after these things he must be released for a little while.

Gehenna—The Lake of Fire

This is the *real* hell. The Lord, Jesus Christ, used the word "Gehenna" to describe the final state of unbelievers. It is an interesting fact that Jesus preached more about hell than any recorded prophet or character in the Bible. The name may be connected to the Valley of Hinnom, a dumping ground for the city of Jerusalem. It was used to burn garbage during the time of Jesus, and therefore was mentioned by the Lord to describe the eternal punishment of those who rejected Him since it is a place of unquenchable fire (Matt 18:8) and was originally created for the devil and his angels (Matt 25:41). It is the eternal place of incarceration of the devil, fallen angels and the unrighteous from Adam through to the Millennium. It is also the final place of separation from God and is described as "the second death".

The Antichrist

The character of the Antichrist is prevalent in prophecy. He is the opposite of Jesus and is a false Christ who rises to power quickly after the rapture. He is the second member of the unholy trinity. He is opposed to Christ and represents everything Christ is not. The prefix "Anti" means "opposed to" or "uncooperative" to Christ. The scriptures tell us that he is a man (Rev 13:18). To understand this end time world ruler, it is always a good start to understand the names given to him.

- The king of Babylon (Is 14:4)
- The little horn (Dan 7:8,24; Dan 8:9,23)
- The king who has fierce features (Dan 8:23)
- The prince who is to come (Dan 9:26,27)
- The king who does his own will (Dan 11:36)
- The man of sin (2 Thess 2:3)
- The lawless one (2 Thess 2:8-9)
- The son of perdition (2 Thess 2:3)
- The beast (Rev 13:2)
- The abomination of desolation (Matt 24:15, Dan 9:27)

Although he is a man, he will appear much more than a mere mortal and will be energized by Satan himself (Rev 13:2). In the chaos implemented by the rapture, many will desire a return to universal stability and will turn to the Antichrist, who seizes this opportunity, and arrives on the world scene negotiating peace programs, also making a covenant of peace with Israel (Dan 9:27). From the on-set, he will be distinguished; for his behavior and charisma will not be like other men. Here is a list of what the scriptures say about this man:

He will be an intellectual genius (Dan 8:23)
He will be a political genius (Rev 17:11-12)
He will be a master of deceitful speech (Dan 7:8)
He will be a commercial genius (Dan 11:43, Rev 13:16-17)
He will be a military genius (Rev 6:2, 13:2)
He will be a religious genius (2 Thess 2:4, Rev 13:8)
He will emerge from a resurrected Roman empire (Dan 7:8, 9:26)

From this list, it is not surprising that he wins the attention and worship of many individuals, yet his identity cannot be revealed until the hinderer—the Holy Spirit dwelling in the church—is removed (2 Thess 2:7,8). Therefore his identity is one of fruitless speculation of which there has been many contentions; one of the strongest being that he is a resurrected Judas Iscariot, since the word 'perdition' is also ascribed to him (Jn 17:12) and since Satan "entered" him just as he will the Antichrist (Lk 22:3, Jn 13:27).

There is currently a heated debate among Bible scholars concerning the origin of the Antichrist. Some hold that he will be a Jew, based on Dan 11:37,38 which declares that he shall not regard the "God of his fathers" suggesting Jewish heritage. Also because he is a substitute Christ, he would have to be a Jew as Jesus was. On the contrary, his persecution of the Jews suggests no affiliation with them. Rev 13:1 portrays him as rising "out of the sea" which is a symbol of the nations of the world, and he is called the "Assyrian" and "King of Babylon" which negates Jewish heritage. Dan 9:28 is another key scripture that refutes the Antichrist being a Jew, for it prophesies that: "The people of the prince who is to come (Antichrist) shall destroy the city and the sanctuary". In AD 70, the Romans destroyed the temple and ravaged Jerusalem; hence the Antichrist has roots in Rome.

He is described as a "beast" in Rev 13:1 to emphasize his tenacious nature, his persecution of Israel and the saints, his execution of anyone who opposes him and his relentless blasphemies towards God. His tyranny exceeds that of any dictator ever known in human history. Hitler, Saddam Hussein, Osama Bin Laden and such will appear as innocent babies in comparison to this monster. Some hold that he will be a homosexual due to this passage of scripture:

Dan 11:37,38
He shall regard neither the God of his fathers nor the desire of women, nor regard any god; for he shall exalt himself above them all. But in their place he shall honor a god of fortresses, and a god which his fathers did not know he shall honor with gold and silver, with precious stones and pleasant things.

His sexual orientation may be a point of speculation for many, but the crux of the passage is that the Antichrist respects no one and gives no thought to sentiments of any kind but is obsessed by war and destruction. He will begin by controlling a federation of nations, which is a new Roman empire. Rev 13:1 describes him as having seven heads and ten horns. The seven heads are seven empires throughout history that have or will persecute Israel, and are: Egypt, Assyria, Babylon, Medo-Persia, Greece, Rome and Reconstituted Rome. The Antichrist's connection to these past nations is a spiritual matter since the one who gives him his power (the devil) used these nations to oppress Israel. The ten horns are the ten kingdoms allied together in the last days and are rulers of the seventh empire—the New Roman Empire. The emergence of the European Union reinforces the unfolding of prophecy in our world today.

He will subdue three of the ten kings in the reunited Roman Empire (Dan 7:24) and the remaining seven kings will give all authority to him. Near the middle of the tribulation, the Antichrist will be violently killed and then he shall be brought back to life (Rev 13:3; 12,4). This act appears to be a counterfeit version of the death and resurrection of Christ, but does seem that the death is an actual death not mere falsehood according to Rev 17:8.

Rev 17:8

The beast that you saw was, and is not, and will ascend out of the bottomless pit and go to perdition. And those who dwell on the earth will marvel, whose names are not written in the Book of Life from the foundation of the world, when they see the beast that was, and is not, and yet is.

It is peculiar that he descends to the Bottomless Pit since the souls of the damned are said to go to hades. However the result of his real/counterfeit death is universal reverence of him. He will invade Israel, he will set himself up in the rebuilt temple proclaiming he is God, which is described by Jesus as the "Abomination of Desolation" (Matt 24:15). During the great tribulation—the last three and a half years—he will be worshiped as God and will work great wonders (2 Thess 2:9-12).

He creates a financial system called the "mark of the beast" in which only those who possess it can buy or sell. Yet taking this mark is certain doom, for everyone who has the mark is considered a worshiper of the Antichrist by God and hence will eventually be cast into the lake of fire. The number of the beast is 666, symbolizing the unholy trinity, which desperately falls short of 777, the number of the holy trinity. Many believe that the mark of the beast will be a microchip, and even more astonishing than that; many prophecy students believe that the Antichrist is alive today, if only as a little baby.

The False Prophet

There have always been false prophets throughout the ages, and in the last days there shall be an abundance of false prophets who will deceive many (Matt 24:24), but one will supercede the rest and rise to the center of the world stage with the Antichrist. He is the third person of the unholy trinity just as the Holy Spirit is in the trinity of God. The ministry of the Holy Spirit is to direct praise and worship to Jesus Christ and to unfold the doctrines of God in a believer's heart and mind, likewise the activities of the false prophet is centered on directing the worship of nations to the Antichrist.

Rev 13:11-13

Then I saw another beast coming up out of the earth, and he had two horns like a lamb and spoke like a dragon. And he exercises all the authority of the first beast in his presence, and causes the earth and those who dwell in it to worship the first beast, whose deadly wound was healed. He performs great signs, so that he even makes fire come down from heaven on the earth in the sight of men.

The first point to note about this false prophet is that the pronoun "he" is given to him, indicating that he is a man. He is called a beast also, impressing a tenacious character similar to that of the Antichrist. Most commentators believe he is of Jewish descent because he comes up "out of the earth" rather than out of the "sea" (the Gentile world). His having two horns like a lamb suggests that he will appear gentle like Christ, the Lamb of God, and may have once participated in the Christian faith but defected. However, underneath the mild exterior he is zealous to speak the words of the devil and speaks "like a dragon". The Antichrist will be primarily a political figure but the false prophet will be a religious figure. The false prophet will be the Antichrist's chief propagandist, his closest companion and his right-hand man, and they will be in perfect fellowship with each other (see Matt 12:25-26). He will do "great signs" while in the presence of the Antichrist, even calling down fire from heaven. It is said that seeing is believing, and he works these signs in the "sight of men" deceiving them into worshiping the Beast, who is the Antichrist. He exercises "all the authority of the first beast" since his source of power is from the devil also, and this phrase suggests a common equality among the unholy trinity that mirrors that of the holy trinity (1 Jn 5:7).

Rev 13:14-15

And he deceives those who dwell on the earth by those signs which he was granted to do in the sight of the beast, telling those who dwell on the earth to make an image to the beast who was wounded by the sword and lived. He was granted power to give breath to the image of the beast, that the image of the beast should both speak and cause as many as would not worship the image of the beast to be killed.

The false prophet erects an image, most likely in the likeness of the Antichrist, which will be the object of worship for the world. Then, incredibly, he gives life to the image so that it speaks. Many prophecy scholars are puzzled by this prophecy because Satan does not have the power to give life; only God does. For this reason it is believed that the image does not actually speak of itself but only appears to do so through deceitful methods or by the advanced technology of our age. The third member of the unholy trinity kills anyone who does not worship the Antichrist. The mark of the beast is administered by the false prophet, which aids the Antichrist in controlling world commerce.

The Dragon

The Book of Revelation does not only reveal the character of God in Christ, but also unmasks the devil for what he really is. He is the epitome of evil; no creature created by God can match the portfolio of diabolical schemes undertaken by the devil since his expulsion from heaven. He is immensely powerful, unspeakably evil and conniving, and lives to destroy and deceive mankind. He is unashamedly persistent in his wicked ways and is in fact the original sinner. Many people disbelieve that there is a devil because that is the greatest lie he has sold to mankind—that he doesn't exist. To believe in the devil is also to believe in the one who created him (God), so some denounce his existence. He is a pronounced liar, Jesus calls Satan a "liar and the father of it" in whom there is no truth to be found in. He is a murderer and holds the power of death (Heb 2:14). He is an abominable creature who roams about seeking men and women to destroy (Jn 10:10).

1 Pet 5:8
Be sober, be vigilant; because your adversary the devil walks about like a roaring lion, seeking whom he may devour.

God did not create the devil, he created Lucifer—an angel of light with a free will. The devil belongs to the angelic class of cherubim since Ez

28:14 describes him as "the anointed cherub who covers". He was at the pinnacle of all God's created beings, an angel perfect in beauty with enormous power and wisdom. Ez 28:15 tell us that Lucifer was "perfect in your ways from the day you were created until iniquity was found in you". At some point, he fell in love with himself because of his beauty and despised his position as subordinate to God and lusted after the title of God himself so he could be worshipped. In Ez 28:17, we are told that "your heart was lifted up because of your beauty; you corrupted your wisdom for the sake of your splendor". Isaiah further explains Lucifer's ambitious yearning to overthrow God.

Is 14:12-14

How you are fallen from heaven, O Lucifer, son of the morning! How you are cut down to the ground, you who weakened the nations! For you have said in your heart: 'I will ascend into heaven, I will exalt my throne above the stars of God; I will also sit on the mount of the congregation on the farthest sides of the north; I will ascend above the heights of the clouds, I will be like the Most High.'

We learn a great deal about the activities and nature of Satan from the various names that are given to him in Revelation chapter 12. He is called:

1. **A great, fiery red dragon** (Rev 12:3). Red signifies danger or fury. He is red because of his destructive nature and his passion to kill men. His portrayal as a dragon is to show the monstrosity of his character.

2. **That serpent of old** (Rev 12:9). This name refers to the form he took to deceive Eve in the Garden of Eden and also exhibits his snaky personality.

3. **The devil** (Rev 12:9). This name means "accuser" or "slanderer" since he accuses those of the faith to God day and night (Rev 12:10) to expose sins or find fault with them.

4. **Satan** (Rev 12:9). This name means "adversary". He is the enemy of God as well as mankind.

In other passages of scripture, Satan is called the ruler of this world (Jn 14:30), the God of this age (2 Cor 4:4), and the prince of the power of the air (Eph 2:2). These scripture verses express the strength, intelligence and ferocity of this creature who is engulfed in an unnatural rage towards God and men. Satan's ultimate goal is to be worshipped, and much of the tribulation directly results from this desire. He even attempted to seduce Christ into worshipping him in the wilderness (Matt 4:9) displaying his absolute disrespect for anything or anyone.

Rev 12:3-4

And another sign appeared in heaven: behold, a great fiery red dragon having seven heads and ten horns, and seven diadems on his heads. His tail drew a third of the stars of heaven and threw them to the earth. And the dragon stood before the woman who was ready to give birth, to devour her Child as soon as it was born.

The passage describing Satan's tail drawing a third of the stars probably refers to his initial mutiny against God, in which he managed to convince a third of the angels to join him in his rebellion. These angels are now called "demons" or "fallen angels" and presently serve the devil. Throughout history, the devil has been seeking the "seed of woman" who was prophesied to "bruise his head" (see Gen 3:15). Women do not have "seeds" so this is clearly a reference to the virgin birth of Christ. When Christ was born, Satan manipulated Herod into the mass slaughter of innocent children in an attempt to kill Jesus, but was unsuccessful. In the future tribulation, Satan will attempt to overthrow God's throne as shown in this passage of scripture:

Rev 12:7-9

And war broke out in heaven: Michael and his angels fought with the dragon; and the dragon and his angels fought, but they did not prevail, nor was a place found for them in heaven any longer. So the great dragon was cast out, that serpent of old, called the Devil and Satan, who deceives the whole world; he was cast to the earth, and his angels were cast out with him.

During the tribulation, just before the great tribulation, Satan will rally his angels to overthrow God and will fight a battle in the heavenlies against Michael the archangel and the holy angels. No one can envision what kind of a war this will be or how it will be fought but the result is that Satan and his fallen angels are cast out of heaven permanently and thrown down to the earth. Apparently, Satan still has access to heaven and frequents it to accuse Christians—demonstrated in Job 2:1, which is how he made the challenge to God that Job would curse Him if the pleasures in his life were taken away. But when he is defeated by Michael and the angels, his access to heaven will be finally stripped from him. Then, being confined to the earth, he takes possession of the Antichrist, enters the rebuilt temple and declares himself to be God. This triggers the "great tribulation". At this point, Satan understands that his time is short (only three and a half years) before his imprisonment and final doom (Rev 13:12) so he unleashes all the wrath in him. Satan's wrath, coupled with God's wrath at this period in the history of man causes this time to be the most awful ever experienced by humanity.

Satan turns his malevolent eyes towards the Jews (the woman who conceives the Christ) and persecutes them severely. The Jews are given "two wings of a great eagle, that she might fly into the wilderness to her place where she is nourished for a time and times and half a time, from the presence of the serpent" (Rev 12:14). The Jews flee for their lives and their speed and ease in which they escape to the wilderness is likened to the flight of an eagle. They will survive here away from the Antichrist. However, Satan is undeterred:

Rev 12:15-16
So the serpent spewed water out of his mouth like a flood after the woman, that he might cause her to be carried away by the flood. But the earth helped the woman, and the earth opened up its mouth and swallowed up the flood which the dragon had spewed out of his mouth.

The water that is spewed out of the mouth of the dragon are armies of the Antichrist whose goal is to overpower the Jews and wipe them out, but the ground they tread upon opens up and "swallows" them—clearly divine intervention from God just in the same way He intervened supernaturally when Pharaoh sent out an army in pursuit of Israel in the days of Moses. This enrages Satan and he oppresses the remaining believing Jews in Israel.

Rev 12:17

And the dragon was enraged with the woman, and he went to make war with the rest of her offspring, who keep the commandments of God and have the testimony of Jesus Christ.

Michael the Archangel

This is clearly an angel with a significant role in the programs of God and even in the last days. He is one of two angels mentioned by name in the Bible, the other being Gabriel, whose role is to deliver prophetic message of God to men. Michael, on the other hand, is portrayed as the leader of God's heavenly army. He is an angel designated for war and a tried and true warrior. He is an archangel, and although in rank he is set apart from the other angels, there may be other archangels in heaven with the same classification. Since we learn that he is able to confront Satan himself, he may also be a member of the cherubim. He is an angel assigned over the nation of Israel, to ensure their protection. During the tribulation, he will become active in this duty.

Dan 12:1

At that time Michael shall stand up, the great prince who stands watch over the sons of your people; and there will be a time of trouble such as never was since there was a nation, even to that time. And at that time your people shall be delivered, every one who is found written in the book.

The name Michael means "who is like God". He will lead an angelic army to fight Satan and the fallen angels during the tribulation. He may even be the angel who casts the devil into the bottomless pit (Rev 20:1) and may also accompany the Lord Jesus Christ to the air on the day of the rapture.

1 Thess 4:16

For the Lord Himself will descend from heaven with a shout, with the voice of an archangel, and with the trumpet of God. And the dead in Christ will rise first.

In the past, Michael helped a lesser-ranked angel to deliver a message to Daniel. The angel had been "withstood" or delayed by demons for twenty-one days until Michael assisted him (Dan 10:13). Michael also disputed with the devil over the body of Moses (Jude 9) but this verse has baffled many commentators because of a lack of details. Despite his great prowess in battle, Michael is humble enough to understand that his power comes from God and rebukes the devil in the Lord's name.

Jude 9

Yet Michael the archangel, in contending with the devil, when he disputed about the body of Moses, dared not bring against him a reviling accusation, but said, "The Lord rebuke you!"

The Twenty-Four Elders

There are numerous views concerning the identity of the twenty-four elders. Some believe that they are angelic beings, others—all of creation, but there are several clues that indicate that this select group is the church. The elders in scripture are representatives of God's people. John the Revelator, even addresses himself by this title in his three epistles, and this is a term of respect used by both Jews and Christians for venerated religious teachers. An elder is one of the faith who has achieved maturity in his walk with God and this is clearly our state as the church when we are raptured, receive our glorious bodies and experience unhindered fellowship with Christ in heaven. The Bible states that creation awaits the revealing of the sons of God (Rev 8:19), meaning that while we are on the earth, even the greatest evangelist or teacher of the faith is a mere child until the day we are changed and taken into heaven to experience full maturity of righteousness and the knowledge of God.

The number is another indicator that the twenty-four elders are the collective body of the church. The Levitical priesthood in the Old Testament was vast in number. Since all the priests could not worship in the temple simultaneously, the priesthood was divided into twenty-four groups, and a representative of each group served in the temple on a rotating basis. All believers in the church are priests unto God (1 Pet 2:9), therefore the twenty-four elders represent the entire church. The twenty-four elders sit on thrones, signifying that they are rulers and have achieved positions of authority. Jesus told his apostles that they would sit on twelve thrones judging the tribes of Israel, and again in Rev 3:21 he promises that whoever overcomes (the world) he will grant to sit with Him on His throne, just as He also overcame and sat down with His father on His throne. This statement is clearly addressed to the church for the next verse says: "He who has an ear, let him hear what the Spirit says to the churches". Rev 4:4 fulfils this earlier verse.

Also, this group wear crowns on their heads, again implying rulership in a shared reign with Christ. At the end of the judgment seat of Christ, believers will receive crowns. The white clothing is the array rewarded to believers redeemed from the earth during the church age.

Rev 3:5

He who overcomes shall be clothed in white garments, and I will not blot his name from the Book of life; but I will confess his name before My Father and before His angels.

Nowhere in the Bible do angels wear crowns. These who are given crowns use them as an instrument of worship by casting them down at the feet of the One who gave the crowns, Jesus Christ, our Redeemer (Rev 4:10). They worship God whole-heartedly for now their redemption is complete. They are located in heaven during the time of the tribulation, emphasizing a pre-tribulation rapture of the church.

The Two Witnesses

These witnesses are the most unusual characters in the end times. Their activities are summed up in one chapter (eleven), which gives us their ministry during the last half of the tribulation. They are people, and more than that, they are prophets, for God calls them "My two witnesses". They will be sent to minister on God's behalf in the midst of the darkness and obscurity on the earth. Having concluded that they are people, the next question is the subject of their identity, which is not explicitly given in Chapter 11 of Revelation. After much contention on the identity of these two witnesses, prophecy theologians have cut the list down to two of three possible people: Enoch, Moses and Elijah. Here is the argument for each of these three men of God:

Enoch. Enoch never died but was taken up to heaven. The Bible says that he walked with God and "he was not, for God took him". Perhaps this is a kind of early rapture experience, but the fact remains that he did not experience physical death. He was also a prophet declaring the judgment to come as surely as the two witnesses to come also will do (Jude 14-15).

Moses. On the Mount of Transfiguration which is a picture of the second coming of Christ, Moses and Elijah appeared with Christ (Matt 17:3) and the idea is that since they are together on this occasion, they may again be together in the end times as the two witnesses of Revelation chapter 11. Moses was a prophet just as the witnesses are, and like Moses in Egypt, the witnesses will turn water into blood and strike the earth with plagues (Rev 11:6).

Elijah. Of all the three, Elijah is the most likely candidate to be one of the witnesses. Like Enoch, he never tasted death but was taken to heaven in a fiery chariot through a whirlwind (2 Kings 2:11). Also, like Moses, he was present at the Transfiguration. Elijah was a prophet just as the witnesses will be, and scripture prophesies that Elijah will come before the great and terrible day of the Lord, which begins at the start of the tribulation (Mal 4:5). He also caused a drought (1 Kings 17:1).

Elijah and Moses appear to be the most likely pair to be the two witnesses because their ministry is like that of these prophets in the last days. However, I personally reject this theory for several reasons. Firstly, the witnesses are not named and so no one knows for sure who they are. I personally believe that Enoch and Elijah may already have a glorified body suitable for them to remain in heaven, and that Moses is in heaven as a spirit since we are told that God buried his body (Deut 34:5-6) and that Michael and Satan disputed over his corpse (Jude 9). My conclusion, as the author of this study, is that the two witnesses are men who have never lived before but are empowered by God in the last days who come in the same *spirit* of judgment and similar ministries as those of Moses and Elijah, since God will not send a prophet in a spirit form or glorified bodies to preach. The fact that these witnesses are mortal also gives backbone to this view.

The two witnesses will prophesy during the tribulation, at the very peak of darkness and devastation, dressed in sackcloth, which are garments of mourning and repentance, and will proclaim salvation and judgment in the midst of an evil world. They are fiery preachers empowered by God to do signs, and may be the instrument by whom the trumpet judgments are administered. As a result of their fiery preaching, they will be hated by the whole world and be severely persecuted. Yet God will protect them supernaturally for the duration of their ministry.

Rev 11:4-5

These are the two olive trees and the two lampstands standing before the God of the earth. And if anyone wants to harm them, fire proceeds from their mouth and devours their enemies. And if anyone wants to harm them, he must be killed in this manner.

The fire that proceeds out of their mouth is clearly literal since the effect it has is death caused by burning. The two witnesses of Revelation 11 will have awesome impact, together with the 144000 witnesses (mentioned later in this book) in producing an enormous soul harvest. However, when their work is done, they will be killed by the Antichrist.

Rev 11:7-9

When they finish their testimony, the beast that ascends out of the bottomless pit will make war against them, overcome them, and kill them. And their dead bodies will lie in the street of the great city which spiritually is called Sodom and Egypt, where also our Lord was crucified. Then those from the peoples, tribes, tongues, and nations will see their dead bodies three-and-a-half days, and not allow their dead bodies to be put into graves.

The witnesses will be nuisances to the kingdom of the devil, and the Antichrist will succeed in killing them. Their bodies will be left in the streets not only as a trophy of the victory of the Antichrist over these men, but as an example to the tribulation believers that resistance to the beast is ultimately futile. The unsaved people of the world refuse the witnesses a decent burial so that their bodies can decay in the streets like dead animals, and they rejoice over the dead witnesses greatly. In fact, they send gifts to one another in celebration of the death of these prophets just as people nowadays do on major holidays, such as Christmas.

Rev 11:10-12

Now after the three-and-a-half days the breath of life from God entered them, and they stood on their feet, and great fear fell on those who saw them. And they heard a loud voice from heaven saying to them, "Come up here." And they ascended to heaven in a cloud, and their enemies saw them.

Let us retrace our steps back to Rev 11:9, which reminds us that the whole world will see their deaths. How can the whole world see the deaths of these two witnesses? Years ago, this prophecy must have seemed impossible to fulfill but technology has improved so dramatically that satellite TV and media allows the world to view any major event that occurs in our generation. So will it be on the day these prophets are killed. Not only will the world watch them die, they will also watch them being raised to life. I can imagine an unbeliever watching the TV screen and gloating over the dead bodies in the streets, then suddenly his eyes pops out and he gasps in amazement when these prophets stand to their feet. Fear will overtake the people of the world for they saw these people die in their sight. The paramedics vouched for their deaths, their decaying corpses grew cold, so how then could they move again? In fear, many will give their lives to God because they also see the witnesses being taken to heaven.

Rev 11:13

In the same hour there was a great earthquake, and a tenth of the city fell. In the earthquake seven thousand people were killed, and the rest were afraid and gave glory to the God of heaven.

The 144000
Jewish Witnesses

This mysterious group of 144000 Jewish people are among the key characters or parties in the end times. They are not the church nor are they the total number of redeemed people throughout the ages. They are a group of 144000 Jewish evangelists, 12000 from each of the twelve tribes of Israel, raised up to serve God during the tribulation. John tells us that God will have a special ministry for these thousands of future Jewish converts to Christ, and that the Lord will prepare their way in a supernatural exercise of divine power:

Rev 7:1-4

After these things I saw four angels standing at the four corners of the earth, holding the four winds of the earth, that the wind should not blow on the earth, on the sea, or on any tree. Then I saw another angel ascending from the east, having the seal of the living God. And he cried with a loud voice to the four angels to whom it was granted to harm the earth and the sea, saying, "Do not harm the earth, the sea, or the trees till we have sealed the servants of our God on their foreheads." And I heard the number of those who were sealed. One hundred and forty-four thousand of all the tribes of the children of Israel were sealed.

God will raise up 144000 Jewish evangelists to travel the globe and rake in a harvest of innumerable souls. These servants will each bear a "seal" on their forehead. It is not clear what this seal is, but it appears to be visible, and is a tag of ownership declaring they are possessions of God just as the mark of the beast shows the Antichrist's ownership over a soul. They will be devoted to serving the Lord and following His commands (Rev 14:4). They will proclaim the gospel of Christ during this sin-immersed era, and will be both persistent and courageous in soul-winning. Their ministry is so effective that they will reach a "multitude which no one can number, of all nations, tribes, peoples, and tongues". They will turn souls from the kingdom of darkness to the light of God's saving grace and instigate the end of the age, since Jesus announced that the end would come only once the gospel has been preached to all the nations of the world.

Matt 24:14

And this gospel of the kingdom will be preached in all the world as a witness to all nations, and then the end will come.

God protects them with the seal he places on them so that they are excluded from His wrath. When the fifth angel sounds the trumpet and the demon locusts are unleashed upon the earth, they will be commanded not to harm the 144000 (Rev 9:4). They are described as 'pure virgins' in chapter 14, verse 4 of the book of Revelation. This could be literal celibacy in servitude of God or may be figurative language to express their spiritually undefiled state.

The Three "Woes"
of Revelation

When the seventh seal is opened in Rev 8:1, which begins the trumpet judgments, there is silence in heaven for about half an hour. I believe that even the four living creatures described in Revelation 4:6-9 keep silent. These living creatures are classified separately from the angels in Rev 5:11 and are therefore entirely different celestial entities altogether who are higher in rank and differ in appearance than common angels. They are not cherubim, despite having bodies that are "full of eyes", since they are described as having six wings and not four and one face each rather than the four-faced cherubim (see Ez 1:5-25 and Ez 10:8-22 for an understanding of the form of the cherubim who are also called "living creatures"). These beings fit the description of the seraphim, as recorded in Is 6:2, with the exception of being "in the midst of the throne and around the throne" (Rev 4:6) rather than explicitly being *above* the throne. Yet, they must be seraphim because it is noted that they "do not rest day or night saying: 'holy, holy, holy, Lord God Almighty, who was and is and is to come!'" (Rev 4:8). However, there is silence in heaven meaning that these living creatures also must have kept quiet at the opening of the seventh seal. The silence in heaven signifies the seriousness, awesomeness and importance of the trumpet judgments. The last three trumpet judgments are described as "woes". These are the ones that shall be the subject of our study. The fifth, sixth and seventh trumpet judgments are so severe that an angel heralds out a preparatory warning cry.

Rev 8:13

And I looked, and I heard an angel flying through the midst of heaven, saying with a loud voice, "Woe, woe, woe to the inhabitants of the earth, because of the remaining blasts of the trumpet of the three angels who are about to sound!"

A "woe" can be described as "doom" and the fact that it is said three times by the angel tells us how many number of "woes" there will be and emphasizes just how terrible they shall be. These last three judgments will be especially horrible because they are directed at the rebellious inhabitants of the earth.

The First Woe

Rev 9:1-4

Then the fifth angel sounded and I saw a star fallen from heaven to the earth. To him was given the key to the bottomless pit. And he opened the bottomless pit, and smoke arose out of the pit like the smoke of a great furnace. So the sun and the air were darkened because of the smoke of the pit. Then out of the smoke locusts came upon the earth. And to them was given power, as the scorpions of the earth have power. They were commanded not to harm the grass of the earth, or any green thing, or any tree, but only those men who do not have the seal of God on their foreheads.

The Bible describes angels as "stars". The angel "fallen" from heaven is not the devil, as some believe, but an angel of God. The bottomless pit or "abyss" is believed to be a place in hell which is in the center of the earth. It is a prison for some fallen angels too vicious to be allowed to roam freely. The angel opens the pit at God's command and fire issues out of the abyss, so much so that the "sun and air are darkened". This is why if I had to describe the tribulation period in one sentence, I would say, "hell on earth"! Once the abyss is opened, all hell breaks loose. The demons are described as "locusts" because of their sizable number and how swiftly they swarm over the earth. In comparison to locusts, however, they do not destroy vegetation but harm degenerate men. Unlike locusts also, these demons follow commands and carry out their tasks strategically. They are commanded not to harm those who have the seal of God on their foreheads.

Rev 9:5-6

And they were not given authority to kill them, but to torment them for five months. Their torment was like the torment of a scorpion when it strikes a man. In those days men will seek death and will not find it; they will desire to die, and death will flee from them.

It is interesting that the sentences "given power", "commanded not to" and "not given authority" are used to explain the activities of these demons. These sentences reveal that at this point they are mere puppets in the hands of God to afflict those who have despised the truth of His Son. Their purpose is to torment and not to kill, and scriptures tell us the duration of their torture—five months. Their tails have stings which they use to menace humanity and the pain they inflict is likened to the sting of a scorpion. It is appropriate that the illustration of the scorpion should be used to describe the ailment of the unrighteous since scorpion stings are rarely fatal but sets the nerves on fire. Anyone who has ever been stung by a scorpion will tell you that it is the most painful ailment you can ever encounter in this life. The pain from these demon locusts is so unbearable that men will long to die. Those who are afflicted will yearn for death to end their torture but it will "flee" from them. Some prophecy students take this scripture passage literally, suggesting that for these five months, death will go on "holiday" as it were, so that nothing done by those who are stung will result in death. But the scriptures appear to suggest that the unbelievers will be in so much pain that they wouldn't even be able to place themselves in a position where they can commit suicide. Let us take the scenario of a man afflicted by these demons who is close to a nearby cliff. He will want to jump off the cliff to commit suicide but will be in such intolerable pain that he wouldn't be able to *walk* to the cliff edge to take his life.

Revelation 9:7-10 describes the appearance of the demons to show that they are neither human beings nor natural locusts. The descriptions of their having "hair like women's hair" and teeth "like lion's teeth" suggest that they have no gender and cannot be resisted nor overcome easily.

Rev 9:11

And they had as king over them the angel of the bottomless pit, whose name in Hebrew is Abaddon, but in Greek he has the name Apollyon.

The fact that the demons have a "king" over them confirms their orderly attack—which cannot be said of natural locusts. "Abaddon" and "Apollyon" means "destroyer" and although this character is thought to be the devil, it is highly unlikely that it is. Why? Because he is called the king of the bottomless pit, implying that he has been an occupant of the abyss and was released, which cannot be said of Satan who will not be imprisoned in the abyss until after Christ returns to the earth at the end of the tribulation. This "king" therefore must be a subordinate of the devil who gives the command for the other locust demons to follow.

The Second Woe

Rev 9:12

One woe is past. Behold, still two more woes are coming after these things.

This verse reads to me like this: "That was just the warm-up session, now let's get down to the real deal."

Are you serious? How much more will the world be able to take? The second "woe" is the sixth trumpet judgment. The angel carrying the trumpet is commanded by God to release four angels who are bound at the river Euphrates.

Rev 9:13-15

Then the sixth angel sounded: And I heard a voice from the four horns of the golden altar which is before God, saying to the sixth angel who had the trumpet, "Release the four angels who are bound at the great river Euphrates." So the four angels, who had been prepared for the hour and the day and the month and year, were released to kill a third of mankind. Now the number of the army of the horsemen was two hundred million; I heard the number of them.

The angels who are bound are fallen angels because good angels are never bound. There is no indication as to why they are bound but they must have committed a sin together or may be too destructive to be let loose. Whatever the case, they are bound at the river Euphrates specifically for a fixed point in God's time-plan. They are released to kill one third of mankind. There is a parallel between this "woe" and the deaths of the first born in Egypt in the days of Moses. God demonstrates his power and reminds us that there is no security for the unjust.

The four angels who were bound lead an army of 200 million—an army sufficient enough to annihilate a third of humanity. Several theologians believe this army are Chinese soldiers, especially since China boast that it can assemble an army of 200 million quickly and easily, having sufficient population to build an army of this number. Alternatively, some commentators hold that since the four angels are demons, the army they commandeer are also demons. The sudden appearance of the army indicates that they may be demons who are also bound with the four angels who lead them.

Rev 9:17-18

And thus I saw the horses in the vision: those who sat on them had breastplates of fiery red, hyacinth blue, and sulfur yellow; and the heads of the horses were like the heads of lions, and out of their mouths came fire, smoke, and brimstone. By these three plagues a third of mankind was killed—by the fire and the smoke and the brimstone which came out of their mouths.

Those who are convinced that this army are Chinese soldiers say that the fire emanating from them suggest nuclear warfare or firearms while those who believe that this army are demons say these demons use the elements of hell to kill mankind. While the locust demons are told not to kill, the purpose of this army is to execute a third of mankind.

The Third Woe

Rev 11:14
The second woe is past. Behold, the third woe is coming quickly. The second woe is the sixth trumpet judgment passed, now the third must begin.

Rev 11:15
Then the seventh angel sounded: and there were loud voices in heaven saying, "The kingdoms of this world have become the kingdoms of our Lord and His Christ, and He shall reign forever and ever!"

The third "woe" is clearly "doom" for anyone opposed to Christ, since He is about to seize the government of the earth from men and will undoubtedly cast out those rebellious to Him. The temple of God opens in heaven indicating that God is about to expel His last and most formidable wrath on earth. The third "woe" is more severe than the other "woes" because it consists of the whole series of bowl judgments. This is a relentless outpouring from the God of the universe.

The Harlot Riding the Beast and the Great City

Rev 17:3-5

So he carried me away in the spirit into the wilderness. And I saw a woman sitting on a scarlet beast which was full of names of blasphemy, having seven heads and ten horns. The woman was arrayed in purple and scarlet, and adorned with gold and precious stones and pearls, having in her hand a golden cup full of abominations and the filthiness of her fornication. And on her forehead a name was written: Mystery, Babylon the Great, the mother of harlots and of the abominations of the earth.

Revelation 17 and 18 describes a great city in the end times called Babylon. Many have speculated as to the identity of this city, some considering it to be New York City since it shall perhaps be the capital of the world. However, the fact that we are given its name several times indicate that it shall be a literal city, and it shall be a rebuilt Babylon. Babylon is mentioned 280 times in the Bible—more than any city except Jerusalem. It is the most significant Pagan city that ever existed, exhibiting a conduct of organized living independent of God. Satan located his headquarters in Babylon and has since began his defiance of God throughout the centuries. It was in Babylon that the great tower of Babel was built (Gen 11:1-9) in which men attempted to reach to God through their own works and earn themselves a name but only succeeded in arousing the anger of God. It is in Babylon that government had its earliest beginnings, eventually producing Nebuchadnezzar, a type of Antichrist who exalted himself in his own sight.

Babylon is located in Iraq and is no longer the great city that it once was, but in the end times it will be a prominent city of the world.

Since the name of the woman is called "Mystery, Babylon" there is a connection with her to this city. This identifies her with the religious practices of ancient and rebuilt Babylon. The woman is the pagan religion that dominates the end time federation of ten nations that makes up this seventh empire or "head" of the beast. The beast empire is ruled by the Antichrist, and for some time, this "harlot religion" will be promoted and practiced by those nations and many nations of the world. Her being adorned with precious stones describes the wealth of this religious practice. She is seen holding a cup; cups in Bible terms symbolize judgment or punishment. Jesus asked for the "cup" of suffering to be taken away from Him because of the brevity of the atonement which would be placed on Him to relinquish the sins of the world (Matt 26:39). The cup is "full" indicating that she is ripe for punishment and she represents everything that is abominable to God.

Although there are similarities between this religious Babylon and the literal city Babylon, they are not to be confused as being the same. Firstly, their names are different: one is Mystery Babylon the Great, Mother of Harlots and of the Abominations of the Earth, while the other is simply Babylon the Great. One is a "mystery" or an object of marvel to John while the other is not. The ten kings rejoice over the destruction of Mystery Babylon but will weep over the destruction of the city of Babylon.

The woman sits on "many waters" and in verse 15, we are told that the waters are "peoples, multitudes, nations, and tongues", meaning that she is practiced by and influences many people on earth. This pagan religion may be a collection of pagan religious beliefs which is "drunk with the blood of the saints and with the blood of martyrs of Jesus". Evidently, she has persecuted many followers of Christ.

Although she is seen riding on "the beast", suggesting a close connection to the Antichrist, she will be destroyed by him as well as the other kings, setting the stage for the Antichrist to enter the temple and declare to the world that he is God.

Rev 17:16

And the ten horns which you saw on the beast, these will hate the harlot, make her desolate and naked, eat her flesh and burn her with fire.

Likewise, the literal city, Babylon, will be destroyed in one hour by God, and the kings and merchants of the earth will weep for her (Rev 18:9-11).

Rev 18:2-3

And he cried mightily with a loud voice, saying, "Babylon the great is fallen, is fallen, and has become a dwelling place of demons, a prison for every foul spirit, and a cage for every unclean and hated bird! For all the nations have drunk of the wine of the wrath of her fornication, the kings of the earth have committed fornication with her, and the merchants of the earth have become rich through the abundance of her luxury."

Armageddon

Several wars will be fought during the time of the tribulation, including the unsuccessful attack of the king of the North and the king of the South against the Antichrist, but at the very end of the tribulation the nations of the world led by the Antichrist will gather at the place called "Armageddon" in the Hebrew to wipe out the Jewish nation once and for all. This is the greatest anti-Semitic endeavor ever carried out in the history of man. For such a great army to gather in this place, the Euphrates River is dried up or altered in such a way as to prepare a path for the kings of the east (Rev 16:12). When the Euphrates river dries up, the devil seizes this opportunity through every means possible—whether by propaganda, deceitful lies, or with false incentives—to stir up the nations of the world against Israel. Their whole attitude shall be like Ps 83 and particularly verse 4 where they are eager to "cut them off from being a nation, that the name of Israel may be remembered no more".

Rev 16:13-14

And I saw three unclean spirits like frogs coming out of the mouth of the dragon, out of the mouth of the beast, and out of the mouth of the false prophet. For they are spirits of demons, performing signs, which go out to the kings of the earth and of the whole world, to gather them to the battle of that great day of God Almighty.

Again, we see the unholy trinity acting as one, sending out demons to deceive the kings of the earth into joining their crusade to exterminate the Jews. This event occurs during the seven-year period of the tribulation in light of its being called the battle of "that great day of God Almighty".

Jerusalem will be attacked and the city falls. Chapter 14 of the book of Zechariah details the events of this invasion with amazing clarity. Let us look at verse 2 to grasp the effect of this invasion.

Zech 14:2

For I will gather all the nations to battle against Jerusalem; the city shall be taken, the houses rifled, and the women ravished. Half of the city shall go into captivity, but the remnant of the people shall not be cut off from the city.

At this moment, the Second Coming occurs. Christ returns to the earth and His feet will touch the Mount of Olives, which splits in two and creates a valley to enable the Jews to flee (Zech 14:4-5). This battle of Armageddon is described as a "great wine press" in Rev 14:19-20, and Rev 19:15 tells us that Jesus treads this winepress of the fierceness of the wrath of God. The imagery of this battle is compared to a winepress because the enemies of Jerusalem shall be dealt with just as grapes are in a winepress in which the juice from the grapes are scattered everywhere. The blood from these armies is so great that it is described as coming up to "the horses' bridles, for one thousand six hundred furlongs". In fact, two scripture passages tell us that Jesus Himself is stained by their blood.

Rev 19:13

He was clothed with a robe dipped in blood, and His name is called the Word of God.

Is 63:1-3

Who is this who comes from Edom, with dyed garments from Bozrah, this One who is glorious in His apparel, traveling in the greatness of His strength? "I who speak in righteousness, mighty to save." Why is Your apparel red, and Your garments like one who treads in the winepress? "I have trodden the winepress alone, and from the peoples no one was with Me. For I have trodden them in My anger, and trampled them in My fury; their blood is sprinkled on My garments, and I have stained all My robes."

Jesus' coming from Edom and Bozrah indicates that the armies gathered against Israel are located in several different places, and that in fact Armageddon is a series of different battles. When Christ comes, He destroys these armies by:

1. A plague (Zech 14:12)
2. A great panic (Zech 14:13)
3. The brightness of His coming (2 Thess 2:8)
4. A sharp sword from His mouth, which are His words (Rev 19:15)

The end result of this great war is that an angel will call all the birds to come and eat the flesh of those who allied themselves to destroy the Jews (Rev 19:17-18). Then the Antichrist and the false prophet will be cast into the lake of fire. Remember that the lake of fire is one of the two eternal states, and that this is not a description of Hades where the present unrighteous dead are at this present moment. The Antichrist and the false prophet are the first occupants of the lake of fire and are cast 'alive' into this place to be tormented forever.

Rev 19:20-21

Then the beast was captured, and with him the false prophet who worked signs in his presence, by which he deceived those who worshipped his image. These two were cast alive into the lake of fire burning with brimstone. And the rest were killed with the sword which proceeded from the mouth of Him who sat on the horse. And all the birds were filled with their flesh.

The Second Coming
of Christ

The Bible is cluttered up with hundreds of verses that insist that Jesus will return to the earth once more. Not only was the first advent (the coming of Christ in the flesh) and His death the crux of the message of the apostles but also that He would come again. Paul also emphasizes this several times and so also do the writers of the New Testament. Let us review one such passage:

Heb 9:27-28
And as it is appointed for men to die once, but after this the judgment, so Christ was offered once to bear the sins of many. To those who eagerly wait for Him He will appear a second time apart from sin for salvation.

In the days of His life on the earth, Jesus Christ Himself declared on numerous occasions that He would return. Here are a few examples of this declaration in the scriptures.

Mark 8:38

"For whoever is ashamed of Me and My words in this adulterous and sinful generation, of him the Son of Man also will be ashamed when He comes in the glory of His Father with the holy angels."

Matt 25:31

When the Son of Man comes in His glory, and all the holy angels with Him, then He will sit on the throne of His glory.

Jn 14:28

You have heard Me say to you, 'I am going away and coming back to you.' If you loved Me, you would rejoice because I said, 'I am going to the Father,' for My father is greater than I.

Jesus is presently with His Father and will return again. At the second coming of Christ, Jesus will come back physically to this earth to judge His enemies, set up His kingdom and rule over the earth for one thousand years. His return marks the end of the age of man's government and Satan's rule, and will usher in the kingdom of God on the earth. During His ministry on earth, Christ Himself did not know when His coming would be. This is because when He chose to become a man, He "made Himself of no reputation" or "emptied" Himself of knowledge and the riches of divinity (Phil 2:7) and we are also told that He "grew" in wisdom, meaning that He was dependent on the Holy Spirit and not on His own knowledge so that whatever the Spirit of God revealed to Him was what He applied, so that He too had to grow spiritually mature day by day just as we Christians do.

Matt 24:36

But of that day and hour no one knows, not even the angels of heaven, but My Father only. But as the days of Noah were, so also will the coming of the Son of Man be.

This passage tells us the conditions on the earth at the time of the second coming—that those days will be just as the days of Noah were before the flood. What were the conditions of Noah's day? The earth was full of violence (Gen 6:11,13), and so also will it be just before the glorious appearing of Christ (see Rev 9:21). The gospel of Matthew also documents the scenario on the earth of which Jesus shall return to.

Matt 24:29

Immediately after the tribulation of those days the sun will be darkened, and the moon will not give its light; the stars will fall from heaven, and the powers of the heavens will be shaken. Then the sign of the Son of Man will appear in heaven, and then all the tribes of the earth will mourn, and they will see the Son of Man coming on the clouds of heaven with power and great glory.

Firstly, we are told that the second coming of Jesus will be after the tribulation and that there would be cosmic alterations of the atmosphere as well as severe darkness. In verse 27 of the same chapter, we are told that His coming will be as lightning flashing from the east to the west—meaning that His return will be obvious to the whole world. This is the greatest prophetic event in history and everyone will witness it. The illumination of His appearing will be so bright that in the darkness of the earth he will be visible to the whole earth. The ungodly who see Him will mourn in despair and those who "pierced Him"—the Jews—will mourn out of sadness for so long rejecting Him (Zech 12:10-12). He will then gather the Jews scattered all over the world who survive the tribulation and bring them into Jerusalem (Matt 24:31). Once He defeats the enemies gathered against the Jews, He will separate the nations of the world into two categories—the sheep nations and the goat nations—according to their treatment of the Jews. The sheep nations will enter the Millennium (the 1000 year reign of Christ) according to Matt 25:34 but the goat nations will be cast into the lake of fire (Matt 25:41)

Matt 25:31-33

"When the Son of Man comes in His glory, and all the holy angels with Him, then He will sit on the throne of His glory. All the nations will be gathered before Him, and He will separate them one from another, as a shepherd divides his sheep from his goats. And He will set the sheep on the right hand and the goats on the left."

Where does the church fit into all this? You may wonder. The scriptures we have reviewed so far persists that the angels come with Christ to the earth at His return, but what about the bride? Has Christ left her in heaven? No, the scriptures say that like the angels of heaven, we, the church, will return with Him at His glorious appearing. Look at these passages that disclose this truth:

1 Thess 3:13
...so that He may establish your hearts blameless in holiness before our God and Father at the coming of our Lord Jesus Christ with all His saints.

Zech 14:5
...Thus the Lord will come, and all the saints with You.

Jude 14
Now Enoch, the seventh from Adam, prophesied about these men also, saying, "Behold, the Lord comes with ten thousands of His saints."

In the glorious appearing of Jesus Christ, He comes to the earth as king of kings and lord of lords with an innumerable procession of angels and believers. It is fascinating to note that the church (those clothed in fine linen) are already beginning to receive special treatment since, like Christ, they shall be seated on white horses. Here is the main passage of scripture in the Bible that shows the coming of our Lord from a heavenly perspective.

Rev 19:11-16
Now I saw heaven opened up, and behold, a white horse. And He who sat on it was called Faithful and True, and in righteousness He judges and makes war. His eyes were like a flame of fire, and on His head were many crowns. He had a name written that no one knew except Himself. He was clothed with a robe dipped in blood, and His name is called the Word of God. And the armies in heaven, clothed in fine linen, white and clean, followed Him on white horses. Now out of His mouth goes a sharp sword, that with it He should strike the nations. And He Himself will rule them with a rod of iron. He himself treads the winepress of the fierceness of the wrath of

God. And He has on His robe and on His thigh a name written: king of kings and lord of lords.

Christ does all the fighting at His return while His procession watches. This advent is different from His first coming in several ways. Firstly, He does not come as a lowly servant but as the God of glory, nor is His purpose to die for the sins of many but to bring resurrection and salvation to His chosen people as well as set up His kingdom on the earth. In His first coming, He made Himself "lower than the angels" (Heb 2:9) permitting Himself to be abused and persecuted in His human flesh despite His supernatural powers, but at His second coming He comes in power and great glory. No longer does He suffer the weakness of men but possesses the authority of God by which power every creature and everything is subjected to Him. Before He ascended to heaven, Jesus told His disciples that all authority in heaven and on earth had been given to Him (Matt 28:18)

The second coming is different from the rapture because Christ comes to the earth to set up His kingdom and not to the air to receive His saints. The rapture is a secret appearance of Christ while the second coming is a public event. In the rapture, He receives the saints while in the second coming He is followed by the saints.

The Millennium

The word "millennium" does not appear in the Bible, but it is derived from two Latin words meaning "thousand years". This expression is used several times in Revelation and should therefore be taken literally. It is the final day. 2 Pet 3:8 tells us that one day with the Lord is as a thousand years, and a thousand years is as one day. God created the world in six days and rested on the seventh day. Since a thousand years is as a day, we have six days of labor (six thousand years) followed by a seventh day of rest; or the thousand-year reign of Christ. There are many discrepancies in history concerning time so no one as yet can calculate exactly when the millennium will begin, but the truth is that it shall be very soon.

Jesus taught His church to pray "Your kingdom come, your will be done on earth as it is in heaven" (Luke 11:2) and this shall come into completion when He sets up the physical kingdom of God on the earth at His return. The government of the kingdom is theocratic because it is a kingdom ruled directly by God in Christ from the throne of David in Jerusalem. His rule will be universal, He will rule with a righteousness and wisdom that has yet to be attained by past rulers. Before Christ begins His reign, he will have a mighty angel bind Satan and cast Him into the lowest depths of the bottomless pit (see Is 14:15) and it is assumed that the fallen angels shall share the same fate.

Rev 20:1-3

Then I saw an angel coming down from heaven, having the key to the bottomless pit and a great chain in his hand. He laid hold of the dragon, that serpent of old, who is the Devil and Satan, and bound him for a thousand years; and he cast him into the bottomless pit, and shut him up, and set a seal on him, so that he should deceive the nations no more till the thousand years were finished. But after these things he must be released for a little while.

With the devil and his angels imprisoned and unable to tempt men into sin or to deceive them into rebellion against God, there will be a time of peace and harmony that will permeate the whole earth. Weapons formally used for war will be reshaped for use in cultivating the earth (Is 2:4) and humanity shall not learn war anymore because the prince of peace dwells with them. The whole motto of the earth will be "holiness unto the Lord". (Zech 14:20-21).

One of the purposes of the millennial kingdom is to restore creation to a quality similar to that of the Garden of Eden before the curse of sin. After the sin of Adam, God placed a curse on the land (Gen 3:17-19) and since the existence of sin there has been earthquakes, hurricanes, storms, volcanic activities and all manners of disturbances which will continue until the end of this age when Christ returns and the saints are 'revealed' after receiving their glorified bodies. The Bible says that just as our earthly bodies have been corrupted and await incorruption, so also has creation been corrupted and await the time when the curse shall be lifted.

Rom 8:19-22

For the earnest expectation of the creation eagerly waits for the revealing of the sons of God. For the creation was subject to futility, not willingly, but because of Him who subjected it in hope; because the creation itself also will be delivered from the bondage of corruption into the glorious liberty of the children of God: For we know that the whole creation groans and labors with birth pangs together until now.

Even animals have been subjected to the curse. Before the original sin of man, animals were tame and peaceful creatures. After the flood, their natures became wild and they hunt each other for food to survive. This will be altered in the 1000-year reign of Christ, for animals will again eat plants only and live together in harmony with each other. Even small children will play with snakes because they shall no longer be harmful.

Is 11:6-8

The wolf also shall dwell with the Lamb, the leopard shall lie with the young goat, the calf and the young lion and the fatling together; and a little child shall lead them. The cow and the bear shall graze; their young ones shall lie down together; and the lion shall eat straw like the ox. The nursing child shall play by the cobra's hole, and the weaned child shall put his hand in the viper's den.

Even wastelands like wildernesses shall "blossom like a rose" (Is 35:1,6-7) and the earth will become amazingly productive so that growing crops etc. no longer requires hard labor. It will literally be heaven on earth during the Millennium. Why? Because the king of creation will be there. It is interesting that a crown of thorns was placed on Jesus' head, since the emergence of thorns and thistles was one of the curses the earth would have to bear after the fall of Adam. I believe that just as His flesh was torn to restore humanity to an untarnished state, so also does the symbol of the curse (the crown of thorns) represent Christ' victory over the corruption of creation.

The duration of the millennial kingdom shall be a time of unprecedented righteousness, joy, peace and knowledge of God (Is 11:9). It will be a time of intense teaching. People who survived the tribulation and were counted worthy to enter the kingdom of God may not have had the opportunity to study the Word during such a perilous time and will require biblical principles for righteous living which may be the role of the redeemed saints and the Jewish evangelists to administer.

All the Jews will be gathered into Israel from the four corners of the earth (Ez 37:25). The Gentile nations (the rest of the world) will be established throughout the whole earth and will live in a similar way to people today i.e. they will work, attend schools, marry and raise families etc. Although these mortals will have some form of self-rule such as governors, mayors or kings, it appears that the redeemed saints will assist in that rule. Remember, there will be two kinds of human beings on the earth—mortals and redeemed man. The mortals are those that survive the tribulation and the children they conceive during the Millennium; and the redeemed are the church, Old Testament and tribulation martyrs. The Old Testament believers and tribulation martyrs will be raised up from the dead at the beginning of the Millennium to rule together with the rest of the saints over these natural men and women.

Rev 20:4

And I saw thrones, and they sat on them, and judgment was committed to them. Then I saw the souls of those who had been beheaded for their witness to Jesus and for the word of God, who had not worshipped the beast or his image, and had not received his mark on their foreheads or on their hands. And they lived and reigned with Christ for a thousand years.

Jerusalem will be the capital of the world, for it is where Christ administers His rulership. Cities are allocated to the saints to rule over based on their levels of faithfulness during their lifetimes on the earth (Luke 19:12-27). The resurrected King David will rule over Israel once more under the authority of Christ (see Is 37:24-25) and shall in fact continue to do so forever into the eternal state. Under David, the twelve apostles will rule over the twelve tribes of Israel (Matt 19:28).

The earth will be full of light during the millennial reign of Christ. How do we know this? Is 30:26 tells us that the light from the sun will be seven times brighter (although apparently not seven times hotter) and that the light of the moon will be as the current light of the sun. Of course, redeemed man is impervious to any conditions, but one has to wonder on the effect of such light on the eyes of the mortals. No one knows the answer as yet but He who created them knows what is best for them. Yet, we are assured that during this one-thousand year period, that the "eyes of the blind shall be opened" and that the ears of the deaf shall hear. In short, there will be revitalization and immense healing to all.

Is 35:5-6

Then the eyes of the blind shall be opened, and the ears of the deaf shall be unstopped. Then the lame shall leap like a deer and the tongue of the dumb sing. For waters shall burst forth in the wilderness, and streams in the desert.

Not much is mentioned of the angels who are said to return to earth with Christ (Matt 25:31) but we are told that they shall be subordinate to the saints (1 Cor 6:3) and to the system of this new kingdom (Heb 2:5). The redeemed are children of God while the angels are servants of God. As heirs, the saints inherit the kingdom and are given the privilege to seat on Christ's throne (Rev 3:2) but the servants (angels) are not given crowns or thrones. And so also shall it be in the eternal state after the 1000-year reign of Christ.

The climate will be warm with uniform temperature. There will be no storms, but there is mention of rain in Is 30:23 and Zech 14:17. The result of the pleasant environment is that death will be virtually non-existent. Natural people entering the Millennium will live for the entire 1000-year period. The earth's population will balloon to a rate of billions, since these mortals retain the capability to procreate, and there will be more people on earth that at any previous time in the past. Ever heard the statement that there will be more people in heaven than hell? The population growth during this kingdom might well fulfill this statement. People will not die of old age nor will there be infant death, but death will still exist although it will be extremely rare. Scripture states that a person who dies at 100 years old would have died prematurely since he would be only a little child, and that a sinner being 100 years old shall be accursed. This suggests that everyone born during the Millennium is given 100 years to make a decision for Christ. If he or she does not submit to the doctrines of righteousness, then punishment will be executed, and in some cases there may be capital punishment dealt out. This is why Christ is portrayed as ruling with a rod of iron (Rev 12:5).

Is 65:20

"No more shall an infant from there live but a few days, nor an old man who has not fulfilled his days; for the child shall die one hundred years old, but the sinner being one hundred years old shall be accursed.

A temple shall be built and many of the rituals of the Old Testament re-instated. There will be animal sacrifices as a reminder of Christ's own self-sacrifice for mankind. Zech 14:17-19 tells us that the feast of Tabernacles shall be observed by the nations of the world at the penalty of receiving a plague and lack of rain for failure to do so.

The Final Rebellion

It is a wonder that even in a near-perfect world sin can still rear its ugly head. This is the reason Christ rules with a rod of iron—because He knows that there are some among the mortals that yearn to be rebellious but will do so only in their hearts until the end of the Millennium. The Bible tells us that Satan will be set free from the bottomless pit near the end of the Millennium, and even goes as far as saying that he *must* be released (Rev 20:3). There is a difference between "will be" and "must" since "must" indicates that God needs Satan to be released for a purpose He has in mind. Many people ask the question: *If God knew that Lucifer would turn evil then why create him at all in the first place?* Here is the answer: because Satan serves the purpose of revealing the true nature of each soul to God and to other men. In simple terms, this means that God uses Satan to test men to see if they will serve Him out of their free will or reject Him. Only under adversity is the character unveiled. How do you know who is a good friend? He is one who is able to support you in times of adversity even at his own expense, but an acquaintance flees when you are in trouble.

So Satan is released, and he reverts immediately to his old tricks again and deceives the nations of the world into rebellion against God. Perhaps, he offers a better kingdom than that of Christ but, surprisingly, he is joined by countless numbers of mortals. They rise up against Jerusalem to fight the saints but are instantly defeated by fire, which falls from heaven.

Rev 20:7-8
Now when the thousand years have expired, Satan will be released from his prison and will go out to deceive the nations which are in the four corners of the earth, Gog and Magog, to gather them together to battle, whose number is as the sand of the sea. They went up on the breadth of the earth and surrounded the camp of the saints and the beloved city. And fire came down from God out of heaven and devoured them.

The devil's demise is fulfilled and he is cast into the lake of fire (the second of the two eternal states) where the Antichrist and the false prophets are. Who says hell is not eternal? The Bible tells us that a thousand years after being cast into the lake of fire, the Antichrist and the false prophet are still there being tormented at the time the devil is also cast in to join them! Jesus Himself over-emphasized that hell was eternal by stating over and over in chapter 9 of the book of Mark that "their worm does not die and the fire is not quenched".

Rev 20:10
The devil, who deceived them, was cast into the lake of fire and brimstone where the beast and the false prophet are. And they will be tormented day and night forever and ever.

The Great White Throne Judgment

Oh man, oh man, oh man, oh man! This is it! This is the biggie! This is the most dreadful event of them all! But let us digress for a moment to a scripture verse that comes to mind every time I read about the Great White Throne judgment.

Heb 10:31
It is a fearful thing to fall into the hands of the living God.

This verse summarizes the nature and purpose of the Great White Throne judgment and gives an accurate portrait of what this event will be like in a single sentence. All those times that you heard of some devious individual not being apprehended for their crimes which made you wonder if God was asleep or oblivious to their wickedness: well here is the due date when these criminals must be brought to account for their vile deeds. This is possibly the most horrific scenario ever described in the Bible, and the most awesome portrayal of the God of judgment of whom we had only previously seen more favorable elements of His character.

Rev 20:11-12

Then I saw a great white throne and Him who sat on it, from whose face the earth and the heaven fled away. And there was found no place for them. And I saw the dead, small and great, standing before God, and books were opened. And another book was opened, which is the Book of Life. And the dead were judged according to their works, by the things which were written in the books.

This is not the judgment seat of Christ, but the judgment of all the unrighteous. This is the place no one wants to be, and the reason why evangelists are fervent in their work to win souls from the darkness into the light of the knowledge of God. Everyone who has rejected Christ as God; those who exalted themselves as God and all manners of abominable people will be present at the great White Throne judgment, but not a single righteous person will be there. These evil people shall partake of the second resurrection, which is the resurrection of the dead unto condemnation. All believers, regardless of their various times of being brought back to life, are classified as partakers of the first resurrection (Rev 20:5-6). We are told that the sea as well as Death and Hades deliver up the dead who are in them. God will gather all the souls of the unrighteous from their imprisonment in Hades, reunite their souls and spirits with their bodies and bring them to judgment from the four corners of the earth. There will be nowhere to hide—which could possibly be the expression that "the earth and the heaven fled away", and there will be no defense, for who can argue with God?

What member of the Godhead is present at this judgment? This is a simple question for we are told the answer in the book of John chapter 5 verse 22, which states that "the Father judges no one but has committed all judgment to the Son". Jesus paid the highest price for humanity and therefore has been given all authority over the affairs of men to decide their fate as He chooses. He is the most qualified to execute judgment on men only in the sense that He is a man and knows the trials and weaknesses of men. Look at this passage of scripture carefully and there will be no doubt in the reader's mind that Christ is the judge at the Great White Throne judgment.

Jn 5:26-30

For as the Father has life in Himself, so He has granted the Son to have life in Himself, and has given Him authority to execute judgment also, because He is the Son of Man. Do not marvel at this; for the hour is coming in which all who are in the graves will hear His voice and come forth—those who have done good unto the resurrection of life and those who have done evil, to the resurrection of condemnation. I can of Myself do nothing. As I hear, I judge; and My judgment is righteous, because I do not seek My own will but the will of the Father who sent Me.

Also, the fact that Christ judges the sheep and goat nations (Matt 25:31-46) and rewards the saints at the judgment seat of Christ is an indicator that judgment is committed to Him and that He will be present at the Great White Throne judgment. This judgment is "white" because Christ judges with holiness, and it is a "great throne" to express the majesty of the One sitting on it. Books, which have records of the life of each heathen, will be opened to show the deeds of every individual, and the Book of Life will also be opened to show the ungodly their omission from having eternal life. This is not a judgment to decide whether one goes to heaven or to hell, it is the place where a sentence of condemnation is laid on the multitude of evildoers present according to their works. There will be a variance in punishment according to each person's application of his or her knowledge of good and evil. Those who are radically evil will receive the greatest punishment—the best example being: the unholy trinity who shall be given the worst of the worst punishment.

Luke 12:47-48

And that servant who knew his master's will, and did not prepare himself or do according to his will, shall be beaten with many stripes. But he who did not know, yet committed things deserving of stripes, shall be beaten with few. For everyone to whom much is given, from him much will be required; and to whom much had been committed, of him they will ask the more.

Death and Hades are thrown into the lake of fire. It is unclear why Death is personified, but Hades—the current place of the unrighteous dead—will be cast into the lake of fire. This sentence reveals that the lake of fire and Hade are two distinct places. When death is destroyed and all the unrighteous are done away with, then the mortals will no longer die and the kingdom will be handed over from Christ to His Father (1 Cor 15:24-27).

Heaven
(The Eternal State)

Rev 21:1

Now I saw a new heaven and a new earth, for the first heaven and the first earth had passed away. Also there was no more sea.

After the Great White Throne judgment, the heavens and the earth are renovated by fire to cleanse them from the curse (2 Pet 3:10). The after-effect will present the earth with an unimaginable beauty that will make the awesome conditions during the millennial reign appear demure in comparison. There will be no thorns, or anything else that is ugly or destructive, and there shall be no more sea, which will enable the earth to accommodate the vast populations of natural men inhabiting it.

Those with natural bodies who entered or were born during the millennium will live similarly to how they lived in the one-thousand year reign of Christ, but nothing is mentioned of their procreating. They shall not age or have their bodies wear out but shall be exuberant and full of vigor, never experiencing sickness or death again (Rev 22:2). Those redeemed from the earth from all ages since Adam will have glorified bodies which mirror the body of Christ after His resurrection (1 Jn 3:2).

They shall not marry nor be given in marriage just as the angels also are (Matt 22:30). Redeemed man shall certainly not need cars during the eternal state—if they exist at all—for they shall travel at the speed of thought: they shall think of a place and be there instantly. Angels ascend and descend from heaven at incredible speeds, and so shall redeemed man also. After His resurrection, although Jesus still appeared mortal (until the dazzle of His ascension), His body had clearly undergone changes, for the scriptures say that He vanished out of the sight of two of His disciples (Lk 24:31) and also that He appeared to His apostles even though they had locked the door for fear of the Jews (Jn 20:19). His sudden appearance terrified His apostles and they believed Him to be an apparition (Lk 24:36-37). This is the same body that the redeemed shall have and we shall do the things that He is able to do, and have access to all of the universe. This is why I often say that we live in the best age—the age of grace—for if you believe that Christ is God then this glorified body shall be yours, there is no "ifs", "buts" or "hows" about it—it shall surely come to pass.

Phil 3:20-21

For our citizenship is in heaven, from which we also eagerly wait for the Savior, the Lord Jesus Christ, who will transform our lowly body that it may be conformed to His glorious body, according to the working by which He is also able even to subdue all things to Himself.

Another element of this glorified body is the light that it gives forth. The transfiguration of our Lord, Jesus Christ, foreshadows His eternal image and that of the saints. He is described as having a countenance full of light that seems like the sun shining at full power (Rev 1:16), and so also shall be the appearance of the Saints. In truth, the redeemed only reflect His light, we know of this because after Moses was with God on Mount Sinai, the Israelites could not look at him directly because of his bright countenance (Ez 34:30) and Moses was compelled to put a veil over his face to speak with them (Ez 34:33). The truth of the radiance of our glorified bodies is found also in Dan 12:3. We shall also retain our identities and the features that we have so that we can be recognized by each other (1 Cor 13:12). There will be no more tears, sorrow, pain or hunger. No more shall we have to go to restrooms to use the toilet or be repulsed by the sight of our own blood!

Rev 21:4

And God will wipe away every tear from their eyes; there shall be no more death, nor sorrow, nor crying. There shall be no more pain, for the former things have passed away.

A beautiful city named the New Jerusalem descends from heaven to the earth. It is shaped like a perfect cube in terms of its length, width and height. It is made up of immaculate jewelry—with each aspect of the city consisting of a certain type of gem. The city has an enormous street made of gold so clear that it appears as transparent glass (Rev 21:21), and a river of life proceeds from the throne of God. The tree of life bears fruit every month for the healing of the nations. This implies that the natural human beings may depend on the tree of life for continued divine health. The most remarkable element of the New Jerusalem is that God the Father will be there and dwell with men.

Rev 21:2-3

Then I, John, saw the holy city, New Jerusalem, coming down from heaven from God, prepared as a bride adorned for her husband. And I heard a loud voice from heaven saying, behold, the tabernacle of God is with men, and He will dwell with them, and they shall be His people. God Himself will be with them and be their God.

The New Jerusalem is laden with "mansions" of which Jesus has been preparing for those who believe in Him. Commentators can only speculate at what these mansions will look like but we are told that "eye has not seen, nor ear heard, nor have entered into the heart of man the things which God has prepared for those who love Him". There will be no temple in this city since it is full of the presence and glory of God, and neither shall there be any night. It will seem as one unending day.

Rev 21:22-23

But I saw no temple in it, for the Lord God almighty and the Lamb are its temple. The city had no need of the sun or the moon to shine in it. The Lamb is its light.

This city will be the capital of the world, and natural man who does not live in this city will be allowed to visit it. The redeemed from all ages will inhabit this city with Christ and govern the whole universe from here throughout all eternity.

Rev 21:4-5

They shall see His face, and His name shall be on their foreheads. There shall be no night there: they need no lamp nor light of the sun, for the Lord God gives them light. And they shall reign forever and ever.

End Notes

The emphasis of the book of Revelation is not only that Christ will return, but that He will do so very soon. From the first chapter, we are told that the "time is near", and Jesus Himself says that not only is His return at hand, but it is "even at the doors". Brethren, these days are coming as certainly as you read this book in front of you, and could even begin this very hour since the rapture is a sign-less event. So many prophesies are being fulfilled in our day and age that we are the generation above all generations before us that can say with more accuracy that Jesus will return in our time. It is believed by many scholars that the generation that sees Israel become a nation (which occurred in 1948) will not pass away before His second coming (see Matt 24:32-35). The countdown begins either when Israel became recognized as a nation in 1948 or when they became in possession of Jerusalem in 1967. All that is left is to figure out how long a generation is in the Bible, which has caused much dispute among prophecy scholars. It does not take even the feeblest mind to realize that we are closer now than ever before. Knowledge has increased, Israel is already on the center stage through global media, scoffers exist, and even a temple is in the process of being built—all signs that reinforces the truth that the age of the reign of the Messiah is upon us.

This may be your last chance at salvation, do not waste this opportunity. Some of the material covered in this book may be unintentionally frightening but there is no need for worry if you trust in the Lord today. Heaven awaits you; the saints of God await you; the New Jerusalem await you; the angels are cheering for you; Christ is knocking at the door of your heart, and God is chasing after you (Luke 15:20). There is no sin that cannot be forgiven by God. Won't you let Him into your hearts right now? The Bible declares that if you confess Jesus Christ as your personal Lord and Savior and believe that God raised Him from the dead, you shall be saved (Romans 10:9). Receive the free gift of God by praying this prayer:

Father, I know that I am a sinner and have sinned against You. Forgive me now and cleanse me from my sins. Jesus, I confess that You are my God who died to take away my sins. Enter into my life now and be with me now and forever. Amen.

Well done! You have passed from death unto life! Welcome into the family of God!